The MAILBOX®

The Education Center®

LANGUAGE ARTS

grades **4-6**

INDEPENDENT PRACTICE SUPER SIMPLE!

144 EASY-TO-USE IDEAS FOR SKILL REINFORCEMENT

 Reading comprehension

 Vocabulary

 Language conventions

 Word skills

 Literary response

 Writing

 Reference skills

 AND LOTS MORE!

ENOUGH FOR
4 activities for every week
OF THE SCHOOL YEAR!

Managing Editor: Peggy Hambright

Editorial Team: Becky S. Andrews, Diane Badden, Brinn Ball, Cindy Barber, Amy Barsanti, Debbie Berris, Brooke Beverly, Kimberley Bruck, Karen A. Brudnak, Sara Chaya Burton, Kitty Campbell, Chris Curry, Colleen Dabney, Dee Demyan, Lynette Dickerson, Juli Engel, Ann Fisher, Theresa Lewis Goode, Tazmen Hansen, Terry Healy, Marsha Heim, Lori Z. Henry, John Hughes, Kathleen Kopp, Debra Liverman, Jeni McCarrell, Dorothy C. McKinney, Thad H. McLaurin, Shawna Miller, Kim Minafo, Sharon Murphy, Jennifer Nunn, Jennifer A. Otter, Mark Rainey, Greg D. Rieves, Hope Rodgers, Kathryn Sandler, Rebecca Saunders, Kathy Scavone, Renee Silliman, Barry Slate, Crissie Stephens, Joshua Thomas, Suzette Westhoff, Zane Williard

www.themailbox.com

D1411347

©2008 The Mailbox® Books
All rights reserved.
ISBN10 #1-56234-842-6 • ISBN13 #978-156234-842-7

Manufactured in the United States
10 9 8 7 6 5 4 3 2 1

Table of Contents

To use the table of contents as a checklist, make a copy of pages 2 and 3. Staple or clip each copy on top of its original page. Each time you use an activity, check its box. Start each school year with fresh copies of the pages.

Skills Index on pages 111-112.

Budding Vocabularies

Synonyms

Materials:
drawing paper
crayons or colored pencils

A student draws on his paper a flower with five petals. He writes an overused word in its center. Then, on each petal, he writes a different synonym for the overused word. If time allows, he turns his paper over and repeats the activity with a different word and its synonyms.

Morphed Words

Following directions

Materials:
copy of the direction cards on page 76, cut apart
paper

A student selects a card and writes an answer on her paper for each step until she changes the beginning word on the card into a new word. She repeats the steps with each card as time allows.

Begin with *MULE*.
1. Insert *BOBBLE* between the second and third letters.
2. Delete the first, fifth, ninth, and tenth letters.
3. Replace the last two letters with *RN*.
4. Switch the order of the third and fourth letters.
5. Add *ST* to the beginning.

Begin with *DAISY*.
1. Insert *LOUD* after the first letter.
2. Move the fourth vowel to the beginning.
3. Replace the second letter with the eighth letter.
4. Replace *O* with the last vowel.
5. Delete the last letter; then change *U* to *N*.

Begin with *PROPER*.
1. Remove both *P*s from the word.
2. Add *ANN* between the second and third letters.
3. Remove the sixth and seventh letters.
4. Replace *A* with *U*.
5. Delete the first letter; then move the last letter to the front.

Begin with *NOTEBOOK*.
1. Delete the first two letters.
2. Replace the second consonant with *A*.
3. Replace the last letter with *R*.
4. Insert *E* between the last vowel and consonant.
5. Replace the double vowels with *CH*.

MULE   Paige
1. MUBOBBLELE
2. UBOBLE
3. UBOBRN
4. UBBORN
5. STUBBORN

NOTEBOOK
1. TEBOOK
2. TEAOOK
3. TEAOOR
4. TEAOOER
5. TEACHER

PROPER
1. ROER
2. ROANNER
3. ROANN
4. ROUNN
5. NOUN

DAISY
1. DLOUDAISY
2. IDLOUDASY
3. ISLOUDAY
4. ISLAUDY
5. ISLAND

All About Me

Similes

Materials:
drawing paper (one sheet per child)
crayons or colored pencils

A student draws a self-portrait in the center of her paper. Next, she adds a web that extends from her illustration as shown. In each circle of the web, she writes a self-descriptive sentence that contains a simile.

Sarah

My hair is as red as a tomato.

When I'm surprised, my eyes get as big as saucers!

My eyes are green like algae on a pond.

My oval face is shaped like an egg.

My freckles look like polka-dots.

I look like a toothpick because my arms and legs are skinny.

Rolling in Details

Sentences

Materials:
magazines
index card labeled with the code shown
die
paper
scissors
tape

A student cuts a picture from a magazine and tapes it to his paper. Below the picture, he writes a two-word sentence about it. He then rolls the die, records the number rolled, and expands his sentence according to the code. He continues in this manner, rolling the die two more times and making the necessary revisions to his sentence after each roll. He repeats the steps with different pictures as time allows.

Code	
	What to Do
Roll	
1	Tell why.
2	Make the verb more specific.
3	Add an adjective or adverb.
4	Make the noun more specific.
5	Tell how or where.
6	You choose what to do (1–5).

Luke

Picture 1
People laugh.
5 People laugh hard.
1 People laugh hard because the man is pulling another man's boot.
3 People laugh hard because the man is pulling another man's yellow boot.

Three to a Column

Spelling

Materials:
copy of the word cards on page 76, cut apart
   and stored in an envelope
10 cards labeled with the vowel sounds shown
paper

A student arranges the vowel-sound cards in rows. Next, he removes the word cards from the envelope. He sorts the words by vowel sounds and stacks them below their matching categories. Then he writes the categories and matching words in columns on his paper and returns the cards to the envelope.

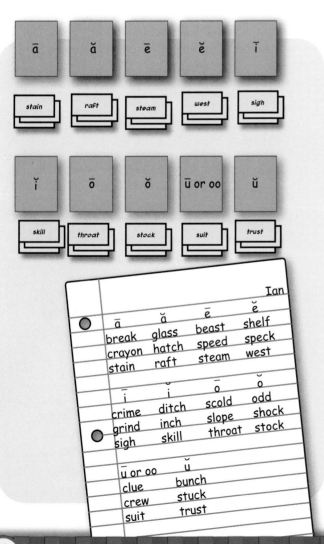

Comic Strip Sequels

Sequential order

Materials:
3 to 5 comic strips, each cut into frames
   and stored in a separate envelope
paper

A student selects an envelope and removes the comic strip frames. She uses the frames' illustrations and text as clues to arrange them in the correct sequence. When she's finished, she thinks of events that might happen if the comic strip continued for three more frames. Next, on her paper, she briefly retells the comic strip's story. Then she writes the title "The Rest of the Story" and extends the comic by adding her own imagined events.

Be the Editor!

Capitalization and punctuation

Materials:
student copies of page 77
colored pencil
paper

A student marks on her copy of the page where capital letters and punctuation are needed. Then she copies the article onto her paper, making the changes she marked.

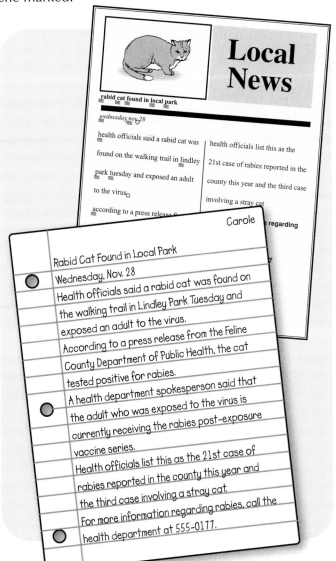

Local News

rabid cat found in local park

wednesday, nov. 28

health officials said a rabid cat was found on the walking trail in lindley park tuesday and exposed an adult to the virus

according to a press release f...

health officials list this as the 21st case of rabies reported in the county this year and the third case involving a stray cat

...regarding

Carole

Rabid Cat Found in Local Park
Wednesday, Nov. 28
Health officials said a rabid cat was found on the walking trail in Lindley Park Tuesday and exposed an adult to the virus.
According to a press release from the Feline County Department of Public Health, the cat tested positive for rabies.
A health department spokesperson said that the adult who was exposed to the virus is currently receiving the rabies post-exposure vaccine series.
Health officials list this as the 21st case of rabies reported in the county this year and the third case involving a stray cat.
For more information regarding rabies, call the health department at 555-0177.

Focused on Structure

Paragraphs

Materials:
sentence strip labeled with a topic
paper
3 crayons or markers (green, yellow, and red)

A student reads the topic on the sentence strip. He writes a paragraph about that topic on his paper, making sure it contains a topic sentence, three supporting sentences, and a concluding sentence. Then he underlines the topic sentence in green, each supporting sentence in yellow, and the concluding sentence in red.

The Importance of Traffic Signals

Evan

Traffic signals are important. Drivers and pedestrians are safer when traffic signals are obeyed. Vehicles stop or move ahead depending on whether a light is red, green, or yellow. People use the signals to know when it is safe to cross a street. Keeping people safe and controlling the movements of traffic are important reasons to have traffic signals.

Make a Word!

Affixes and base words

Materials:
tagboard copy of the puzzle cards from page 78,
   cut into pieces
paper
dictionary

   A student finds three pieces that form a word when assembled. He checks the dictionary to verify the word's spelling and then records the word on his paper. He continues in this manner until he has recorded all 15 words.

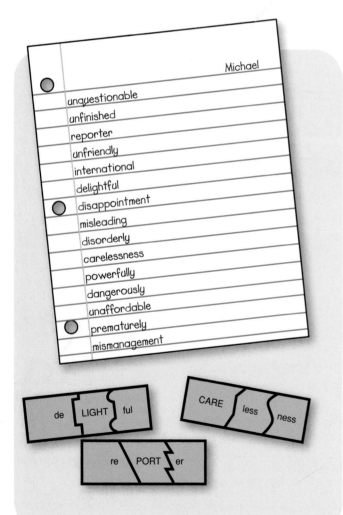

Choose From the Cube

Story elements

Materials:
cube-shaped tissue box, wrapped in paper and
   labeled with story elements
paper

> Possible story elements include characters, setting, problem and how it was solved, main events, point of view, and theme.

   A student rolls the cube to choose three different story elements. She then writes on her paper a paragraph identifying the selected elements in a book or story she recently read.

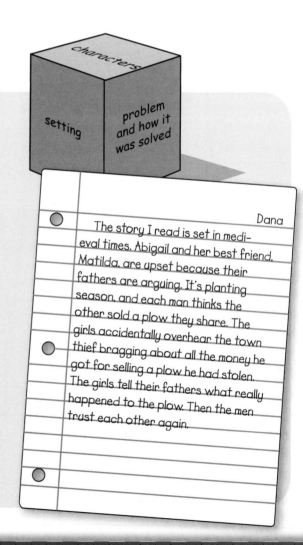

Make a Match!

Contractions

Materials:
2 different-colored sets of circle cutouts: one color labeled with contractions and the other with the words the contractions represent
paper

A student matches each contraction to the two words that are combined to form it and writes her answer on her paper. After she records all the matches, she writes a sentence using each contraction.

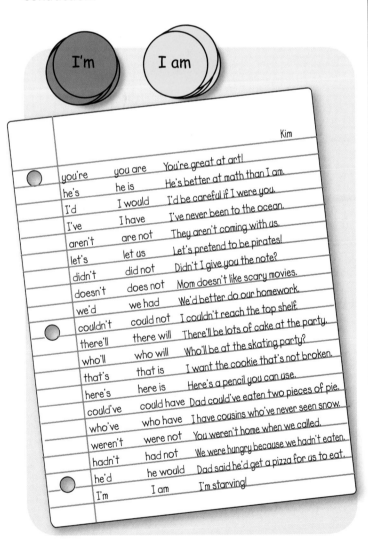

Give Them a Hand

Paragraphs

Materials:
list of topics, like the one shown
large sheet of construction paper (one per student)
scissors

A student draws a giant hand on his paper. Next, he chooses a paragraph topic from the list and writes it on the palm of his drawing. On the drawing's thumb, he writes the first sentence of his paragraph. On each of the drawing's next three fingers, he writes a supporting sentence. He writes a concluding sentence on the drawing's pinkie finger. Then he cuts out the shape.

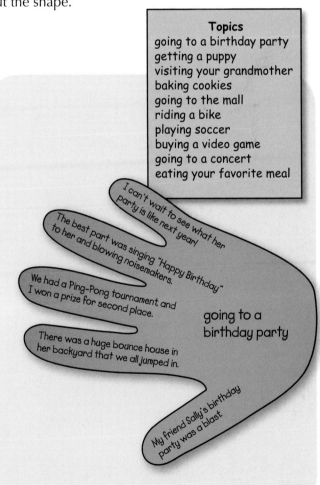

Word in the Spotlight

Vocabulary

Materials:
student copies of the recording sheet on page 78
sentence strip labeled with an unfamiliar word
dictionary
thesaurus

A student copies the vocabulary word onto a copy of the recording sheet. Then he uses the dictionary and thesaurus to complete the page. If desired, laminate a blank sentence strip and label it with a different word each week.

Five Ws Star

Summarizing

Materials:
newspaper or picture books
sheet of yellow construction paper (one per student)
scissors

A student draws a large star on her paper. Next, she selects a newspaper article or a picture book and writes its title in the center of her star. After she reads her selection, she labels each point of her star with a different question, as shown, and answers the questions. Then she cuts out the star and writes on the back a sentence that summarizes what she read.

Comma Checkup

Punctuation

Materials:
laminated sentence strips, each labeled with
    a sentence that needs commas
paper
wipe-off marker

A student selects a sentence strip and uses the marker to add commas where they are needed. Then she writes the sentence correctly on her paper. She repeats the steps, using a different sentence strip each time, as time allows.

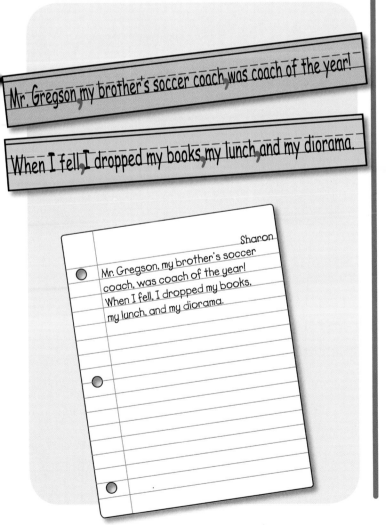

Mr. Gregson, my brother's soccer coach, was coach of the year!

When I fell, I dropped my books, my lunch, and my diorama.

Sharon

Mr. Gregson, my brother's soccer coach, was coach of the year!
When I fell, I dropped my books, my lunch, and my diorama.

Dear Teacher

Friendly letter

Materials:
newspaper
poster board programmed with the format of
    a friendly letter
paper

A student finds in the newspaper an interesting article about a current event. Then, using the format on the poster as a guide, he writes his teacher a letter about the selected event.

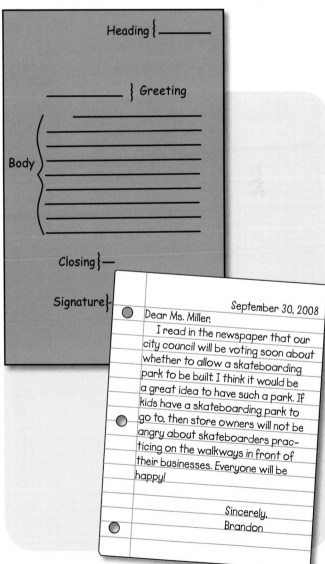

Heading {———

———— } Greeting

Body {

Closing }—

Signature}—

September 30, 2008

Dear Ms. Miller,
    I read in the newspaper that our city council will be voting soon about whether to allow a skateboarding park to be built. I think it would be a great idea to have such a park. If kids have a skateboarding park to go to, then store owners will not be angry about skateboarders practicing on the walkways in front of their businesses. Everyone will be happy!

Sincerely,
Brandon

Two's the Clue

Suffixes

Materials:
copy of the silent *e* word list on page 79
copy of the list of suffixes on page 79
construction paper sign labeled as shown
paper

A student chooses ten or more words from the list and writes them on his paper. Next, he chooses a suffix to add to each word. Then he uses the message on the sign to help him write the correct spelling of each word.

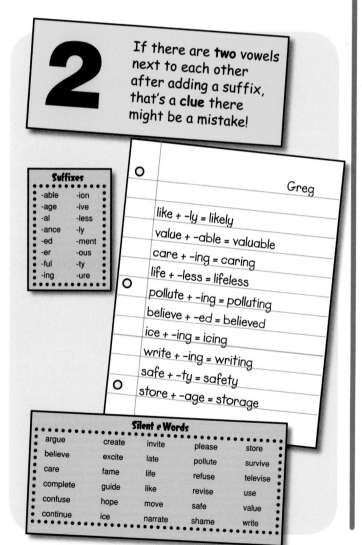

2
If there are **two** vowels next to each other after adding a suffix, that's a **clue** there might be a mistake!

Suffixes

-able	-ion
-age	-ive
-al	-less
-ance	-ly
-ed	-ment
-er	-ous
-ful	-ty
-ing	-ure

Greg

like + -ly = likely
value + -able = valuable
care + -ing = caring
life + -less = lifeless
pollute + -ing = polluting
believe + -ed = believed
ice + -ing = icing
write + -ing = writing
safe + -ty = safety
store + -age = storage

Silent e Words

argue	create	invite	please	store
believe	excite	late	pollute	survive
care	fame	life	refuse	televise
complete	guide	like	revise	use
confuse	hope	move	safe	value
continue	ice	narrate	shame	write

What's Happening?

Inference

Materials:
3 to 5 comic strips (with text whited out), each mounted on a numbered sheet of paper
paper

A student selects a comic strip and studies its illustrations. Then she writes on her paper what she thinks the comic strip is about. She repeats the steps with each comic strip.

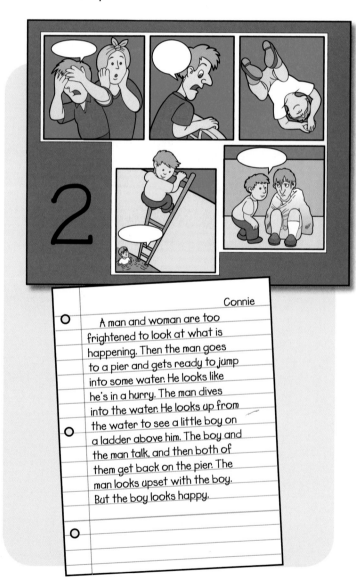

Connie

A man and woman are too frightened to look at what is happening. Then the man goes to a pier and gets ready to jump into some water. He looks like he's in a hurry. The man dives into the water. He looks up from the water to see a little boy on a ladder above him. The boy and the man talk, and then both of them get back on the pier. The man looks upset with the boy. But the boy looks happy.

Picture Prompts

Types of sentences

Materials:
pictures from magazines or old books, numbered paper

A student selects a picture. Then he writes on his paper four sentences (one declarative, one interrogative, one exclamatory, and one imperative) about each picture. He repeats the steps with two more pictures until he has written 12 sentences in all.

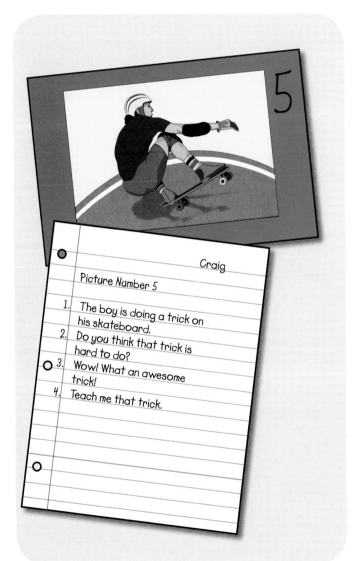

Craig

Picture Number 5

1. The boy is doing a trick on his skateboard.
2. Do you think that trick is hard to do?
3. Wow! What an awesome trick!
4. Teach me that trick.

Let's Be Sensible

Descriptive writing

Materials:
magazines
colorful paper (one sheet per student)
scissors
glue

A student cuts a picture from a magazine and glues the picture at the top of a sheet of paper. Then, using her senses, she writes on the paper a paragraph that vividly describes the pictured image.

Amy

I love standing on a warm sandy beach and feeling gritty pieces of sand between my toes. The salty spray from thundering waves splashes on my face and makes me blink. Behind me, I hear the soft rustling sounds of palm trees swaying gently in the wind. I close my eyes and take a deep breath of refreshing ocean air. What a moment!

Show the Opposite

Antonyms

Materials:
drawing paper (one sheet per student)
crayons

A student folds his paper in half and then unfolds it. On the top left side of the paper, he writes a sentence that contains a word for which there is an antonym. On the top right side, he writes the same sentence but replaces that word with an appropriate antonym. Then he illustrates each sentence.

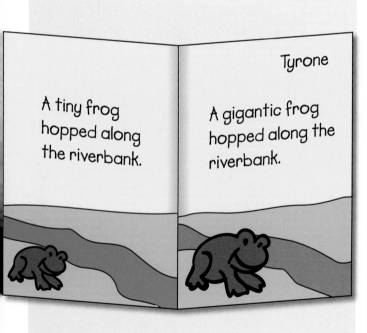

Important Information

Text features

Materials:
page protectors, each filled with a nonfiction selection that has several text features
unlined paper (one sheet per student)

A student folds her paper into fourths, unfolds the paper, and labels its sections as shown. Next, she picks a selection and, based on its title, writes in her paper's first section a sentence telling what she thinks the selection will be about. Then she reads the selection and writes in the second section a sentence telling something she learned from the illustrations. In the third section, she writes a sentence telling something she learned from the other features listed. In the last section, she writes two sentences telling what she learned solely from the selection's text.

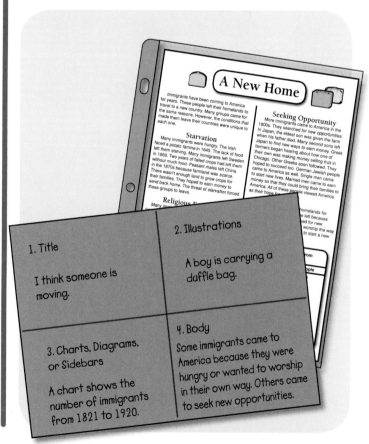

Color-Code It!

Apostrophes

Materials:
copy of page 80 inside a page protector
red and blue wipe-off markers

A student reads each sentence and decides how each apostrophe is used. If it shows possession, he circles it in red. If it indicates one or more missing letters in a contraction, he circles it in blue.

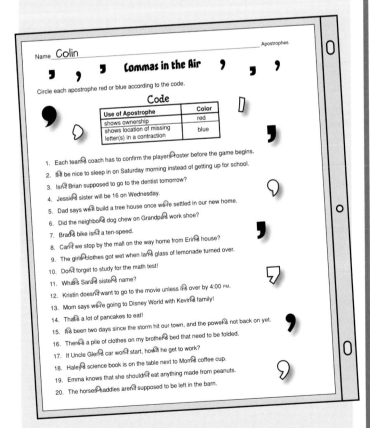

Name Colin   Apostrophes

Commas in the Air

Circle each apostrophe red or blue according to the code.

Code

Use of Apostrophe	Color
shows ownership	red
shows location of missing letter(s) in a contraction	blue

1. Each team's coach has to confirm the players' roster before the game begins.
2. It'll be nice to sleep in on Saturday morning instead of getting up for school.
3. Isn't Brian supposed to go to the dentist tomorrow?
4. Jessie's sister will be 16 on Wednesday.
5. Dad says we'll build a tree house once we're settled in our new home.
6. Did the neighbor's dog chew on Grandpa's work shoe?
7. Brad's bike isn't a ten-speed.
8. Can't we stop by the mall on the way home from Erin's house?
9. The girls' clothes got wet when Ian's glass of lemonade turned over.
10. Don't forget to study for the math test!
11. What's Sara's sister's name?
12. Kristin doesn't want to go to the movie unless it's over by 4:00 PM.
13. Mom says we're going to Disney World with Kevin's family!
14. That's a lot of pancakes to eat!
15. It's been two days since the storm hit our town, and the power's not back on yet.
16. There's a pile of clothes on my brother's bed that need to be folded.
17. If Uncle Glenn's car won't start, how'll he get to work?
18. Haley's science book is on the table next to Mom's coffee cup.
19. Emma knows that she shouldn't eat anything made from peanuts.
20. The horses' saddles aren't supposed to be left in the barn.

Picture-Perfect Story

Beginning, middle, and end

Materials:
calendar or magazine pictures
index cards (three per student)
tape

A student selects a picture. On one index card, she writes a paragraph about the pictured event. On the second index card, she writes a paragraph about an event that could have happened just before the event in the picture. On the third index card, she writes a paragraph about an event that could have happened just after the event in the picture. Then she tapes the cards together in order vertically as shown.

Caroline

It is just an ordinary summer day for the honeybees, buzzing from flower to flower. Suddenly, something red catches one bee's eye. The bee flies closer and sees that the red thing is on a picnic table.

A father, a mother, and two children are eating a picnic lunch under a big shade tree. They are talking and laughing as they eat. None of them seem to notice that a bee has just landed on a big slice of watermelon.

All at once, the bee feels something swooping in its direction. Just in time, it looks to see a folded newspaper in the man's hand. Instantly, the bee knows it has to fly away fast. It quickly takes a teeny sip of red liquid and then makes a beeline for the nearest flower. It is a close call, but the bee thinks that small sip of watermelon juice was well worth the risk!

Terrific Title

Alliteration

Materials:
magazines
construction paper (one sheet per student)
markers
scissors
glue
tape
paper

A student finds a picture in a magazine. He cuts out the picture and glues it to construction paper, leaving room to write a title. He thinks of a clever title that uses alliteration and adds it to the construction paper. On another sheet of paper, he uses the title to write a paragraph or poem and tapes it to the construction paper.

Toddler Trouble

What's a dad to do
When his quadruplets look the same?
If he's smart, he grabs a pen
And on the diapers he writes their
     names!

Josh

What and Why?

Cause and effect

Materials:
magazines or old calendars with pictures
construction paper (one sheet per student)
markers
scissors
glue

A student cuts out a picture, glues it to the left side of her construction paper, and writes "Cause" above it. She then writes "so" to the right of the picture and draws three lines as shown. Below the picture, she writes a sentence telling what the picture shows. On each branch, she writes a different effect to go along with the picture.

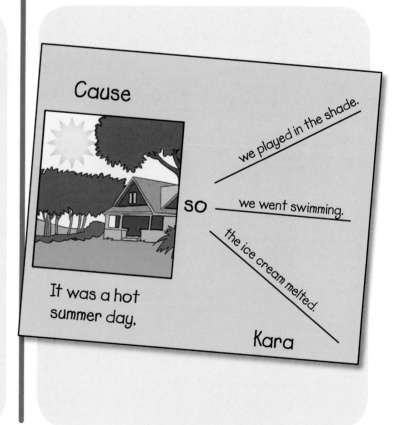

Cause

so — we played in the shade.

we went swimming.

the ice cream melted.

It was a hot summer day.

Kara

Fan Them Out

Sentence fragments

Materials:
newspapers, advertising circulars, or magazines
unlined paper (one sheet per student)
scissors
glue
stapler

A student accordion-folds his paper. Next, he cuts sentence fragments from the sources and glues a different cutout to every other section. On the section below each cutout, he rewrites the fragment as a complete sentence. If desired, he decorates the fan with markers. He completes his fan by stapling together the folds at one end.

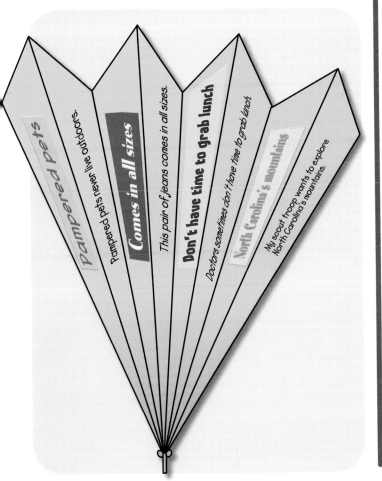

Tell a Tale

Story mapping

Materials:
student copies of page 81
paper

A student plans an original story by labeling the corresponding boxes on her page with three different events, a climax, and a resolution. Then, using her organizer as a guide, she writes on another sheet of paper a story that includes the elements on her map.

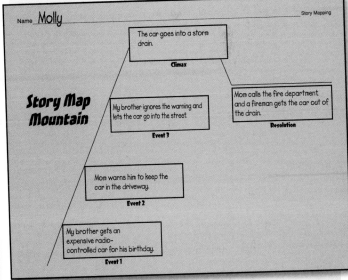

Set 8

"Spider-ific" Words

Synonyms

Materials:
student copies of the spider pattern on page 79
thesaurus
gray or brown crayon
scissors

A student cuts out a spider. Next, he writes on the cutout's body a vocabulary word from a story being read or a topic being studied. On each leg of the cutout, he writes a different synonym for the vocabulary word. He labels as many legs as possible, using the thesaurus for help if needed. He then lightly colors his cutout.

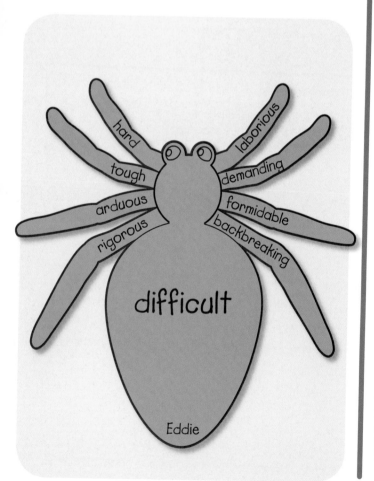

Make a Chain

Making connections

Materials:
children's magazines or picture books
construction paper strips (blue, yellow, and green)
glue

A student reads a self-selected article or short story. As she reads, she jots text-to-self connections on yellow strips, text-to-text connections on blue strips, and text-to-world connections on green strips. When she's finished, she uses the glue to form a paper chain with the strips.

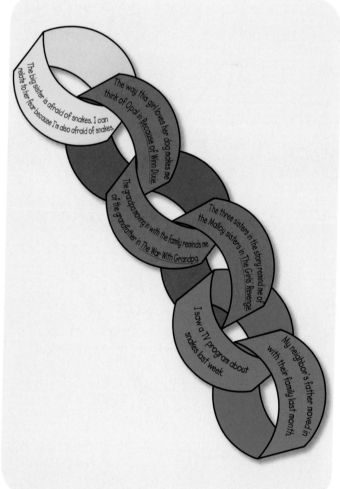

Whose Job?

Punctuating dialogue

Materials:
list of opposing characters, as shown
crayons or colored pencils
paper

A student chooses a set of opposing characters from the list. He writes a conversation between the two characters in which each character tries to convince the other that it is more important. Then he illustrates his work.

Opposing Characters

fork and spoon
dog and cat
sun and moon
pencil and pen

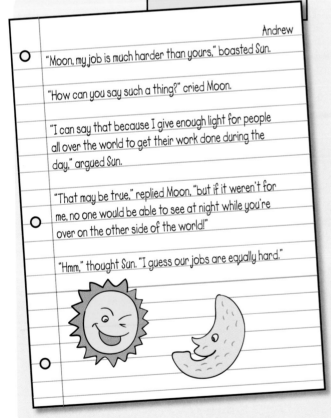

Andrew

"Moon, my job is much harder than yours," boasted Sun.

"How can you say such a thing?" cried Moon.

"I can say that because I give enough light for people all over the world to get their work done during the day," argued Sun.

"That may be true," replied Moon, "but if it weren't for me, no one would be able to see at night while you're over on the other side of the world!"

"Hmm," thought Sun. "I guess our jobs are equally hard."

"Cell-ebrate"

Personal narrative

Materials:
student copies of page 82
lined paper (two to three sheets per student)
scissors
stapler
crayons or colored pencils

A student cuts out a cell phone pattern. In the phone's display screen, she illustrates an event she is anxious to tell a friend about. Next, she traces the cutout onto her paper several times and cuts out the tracings. She creates a minibooklet by stapling the trimmed pages behind the cell phone cutout. On the trimmed pages, she writes about the event she illustrated.

An Unexpected Surprise
As I walked into the mall today, I never thought I'd be getting the surprise of my life!
Mom and I were just finishing our shopping when I suggested that we get ice cream to eat on the way home. We waited in line behind two other people. Then, when they stepped away, I went up to place our order.
All at once, bells started ringing and horns started blaring. The people working behind the counter all had startled looks on their faces.
"What's happening?" I asked.
Before any of the workers could answer, the manager came running out of his office with a big smile on his face. He was carrying balloons in one hand and a small piece of plastic

Sale of the Century

Irregular plurals

Materials:
student copies of the online catalog form on page 83
list of nouns with irregular plurals, as shown

A student chooses an item (noun) from the list. Next, he writes on a copy of the form a descriptive catalog entry for the selected item, making sure to include the item's singular and plural forms. The child then completes the entry with the sale prices for one, two, or three items.

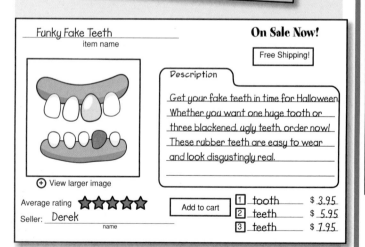

Nouns

bus	mouse
cactus	oasis
calf	octopus
fish	ox
fungus	scarf
goose	sheep
hippopotamus	shelf
leaf	tooth
loaf	watch
moose	wolf

Funky Fake Teeth
item name

On Sale Now!

Free Shipping!

Description

Get your fake teeth in time for Halloween. Whether you want one huge tooth or three blackened, ugly teeth, order now! These rubber teeth are easy to wear and look disgustingly real.

⊕ View larger image

Average rating ★★★★★

Seller: _Derek_
name

Add to cart

1	tooth	$ 3.95
2	teeth	$ 5.95
3	teeth	$ 7.95

Short Story Sort

Sequencing

Materials:
student copies of page 84
scissors
stapler

A student cuts apart the cards. Next, she reads the cards and stacks them sequentially to tell the story shown below. Then she staples the cards together, as shown, to make a minibooklet.

Spunky was born in the back of a pickup truck. Luckily, the truck had no tires, so it wasn't going anywhere. Spunky had four sisters and three brothers. Spunky was the runt: the tiniest, weakest puppy in the litter.

She was spunky though. That's how she got her name. When it was time to eat, Spunky's brothers and sisters pushed her out of the way. So Spunky wiggled. Spunky squirmed. Spunky made room for herself. Before long, Spunky wasn't the tiniest or the weakest puppy in the litter.

It was a good thing she was spunky too. One morning, Spunky caught sight of a bumblebee. It buzzed by her one time, two times, three times. She watched the bee, she snapped at the bee, and then she chased the bee. Before she knew what had happened, she had chased the bee right off the back of the truck.

Spunky tumbled when she hit the ground, rolling over and over. When she finally quit rolling, she was dizzy and tangled up in tumbleweeds. Spunky shook her head, looked around, and pawed her way out of the thorny bushes. She couldn't see the bee, the truck, or her family.

Spunky whined for a minute. She sniffed. She ran to the other side of the tumbleweeds. She looked around. She sniffed. She whined. She dug a little hole and lay down in the cool dirt. Spunky whimpered; then she closed her eyes and fell asleep.

After a while, Spunky smelled a familiar smell. She felt familiar kisses. She heard a reassuring groan. Spunky opened one eye and looked around. She sniffed. It wasn't a dream. It was her mom. Spunky was safe, and her mother realized it was time to move her puppies. It was time to move out of the back of the pickup truck. It was time to move to the ground where all the puppies could safely chase bumblebees and each other.

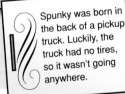

Spunky was born in the back of a pickup truck. Luckily, the truck had no tires, so it wasn't going anywhere.

Rolling Grammar

Subjects and predicates

Materials:
10 index cards, each labeled with a complex sentence
die

A student takes the first card and rolls the die. If the child rolls an even number, he records the sentence's subject. If the child rolls an odd number, he records the sentence's predicate. He repeats the process for each card.

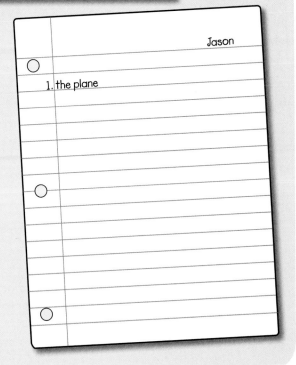

Open Up!

Paragraphs

Materials:
student copies of the skydiver organizer from page 83
list of writing topics as shown

A student chooses a topic from the list and writes it on a copy of page 83. Next, she writes a topic sentence on the parachute. Then she lists in each section under the parachute a sentence that supports the topic sentence.

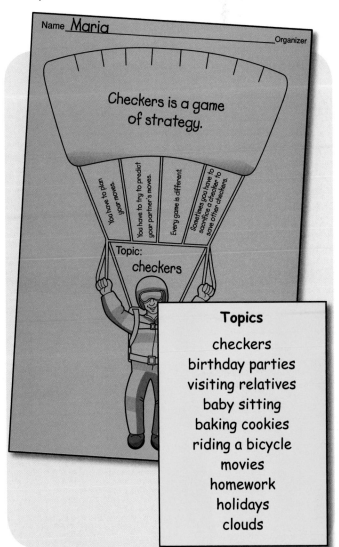

Topics

checkers
birthday parties
visiting relatives
baby sitting
baking cookies
riding a bicycle
movies
homework
holidays
clouds

Word Pairs

Homophones

Materials:
newspapers, magazines, or old books
homophone list (see below)
construction paper (one sheet per student)
scissors
glue

A student folds a sheet of construction paper into four sections. Next, he chooses four homophone pairs from the list. Then he cuts out a picture that illustrates each word. He glues each set of pictures in a different section and then labels each picture.

Homophones

ate, eight	muscle, mussel
blew, blue	oar, ore
board, bored	one, won
brake, break	pain, pane
capital, capitol	pair, pear
cents, sense	plain, plane
flea, flee	prince, prints
flew, flu	right, write
heal, heel	ring, wring
heard, herd	sail, sale
hole, whole	sea, see
knight, night	soar, sore
mail, male	some, sum

Payton

pair   pear   blue   blew

pain   pane   right   write

Noteworthy Ideas

Main idea

Materials:
student copies of page 85
children's magazines

A student chooses a magazine article with at least three paragraphs. She reads the article and identifies each paragraph's main idea. Then she completes the outline, listing the main ideas and supporting details for three paragraphs.

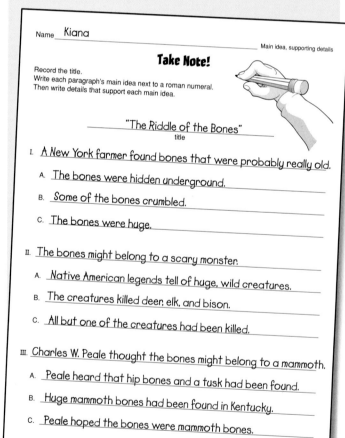

Name Kiana

Main idea, supporting details

Take Note!

Record the title.
Write each paragraph's main idea next to a roman numeral.
Then write details that support each main idea.

"The Riddle of the Bones"
title

I. A New York farmer found bones that were probably really old.
   A. The bones were hidden underground.
   B. Some of the bones crumbled.
   C. The bones were huge.

II. The bones might belong to a scary monster.
   A. Native American legends tell of huge, wild creatures.
   B. The creatures killed deer, elk, and bison.
   C. All but one of the creatures had been killed.

III. Charles W. Peale thought the bones might belong to a mammoth.
   A. Peale heard that hip bones and a tusk had been found.
   B. Huge mammoth bones had been found in Kentucky.
   C. Peale hoped the bones were mammoth bones.

Fill-in Fun

Sentences

Materials:
noun list
verb list
4 sheets of chart paper labeled as shown

A student chooses a noun and a verb from the lists. On the declarative sentences chart, he writes a statement using his selected noun as the subject and his selected verb as the predicate. He uses the same subject and predicate to write a question, a command, and an exclamation on the corresponding charts.

Nouns	Verbs
fox	crash
astronaut	burst
polar bear	float
student	dive
athlete	think
diver	open
backpack	creep
thunder	leap
musician	tumble
	serenade

Declarative Sentences
1. My backpack tumbled onto the floor.

Interrogative Sentences
1. Why did my backpack tumble onto the floor?

Imperative Sentences
1. Backpack, do not tumble onto the floor again.

Exclamatory Sentences
1. Oh, my backpack tumbled onto the floor!

Check!

Editing

Materials:
copies of students' writing samples, cut into
    sentence or paragraph strips
colored pencils
chart of editing marks

A student chooses a strip and a colored pencil. She jots her name on the strip and then uses editing marks to identify any errors. She edits additional strips as time allows.

Editing Marks	
capital letter	≡
lowercase letter	lc
indent paragraph	¶
check spelling	◯
insert	^
delete	ℯ

✔ed by DeAnna

¶ I work with my horse (evryday) after school. I have to make sure she has enough hay, and that her water is fresh. After that, I train her how to jump. She practices jumping Obstacles without me. Then I get to ride her, and we practice jumping together.

As Tasty as Candy

Similes

Materials:
grocery advertisements
sticky notes

A student skims the advertisements and thinks of similes to describe featured items. He writes each simile on a sticky note, adds his initials, and places it beside the matching item.

What If...?

Comprehension

Materials:
copies of 86, cut out
4 or more fiction picture books
blank paper
glue

A student chooses two books to read. When she is finished reading, she chooses a paper slip, glues it to a sheet of paper, and records her response. If time allows, she chooses and responds to additional slips.

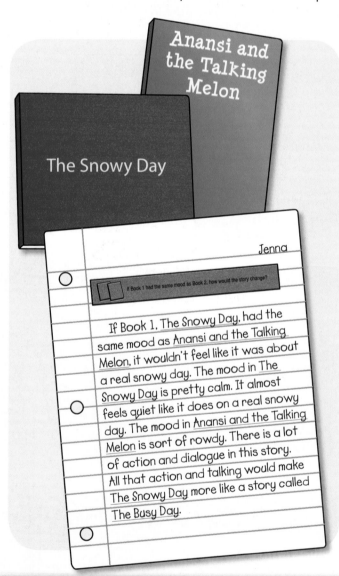

He or Him?

Nouns, pronouns

Materials:
student copies of page 87
scissors
glue

A student cuts apart the noun and pronoun cards at the bottom of his page. Then he arranges the nouns and pronouns in the page's boxes, making sure each pronoun correctly renames a preceding noun. When the paragraph is complete, the student glues each card in place.

Shrinking Notes

Summarizing

Materials:
children's magazine
large index cards (one per student)
small index cards (one per student)
sticky notes (one per student)

A student chooses and then reads an article from the magazine. As the child reads, she notes important details on the large index card. Next, she rereads her notes, identifies the main idea, and writes it on the small index card. She adds two to three supporting details. Then the student rereads the small card and revises her writing to create a brief summary that fits on the sticky note.

Name __Natalie__

Cut apart the cards at the bottom of the page.
Glue each card in a box below to complete the paragraph.

Late Again!

Nouns, pronouns

When [John] missed the bus this morning, [he] knew [his] parents would be mad at [him]. John had already missed the bus two times this week! John's [parents] told [him] [they] would not drive [him] to school if [John] missed the bus again. So [John] started walking. [He] walked to the home of [his] aunt and uncle. [John] was pretty sure his [aunt] would drive [him] to school if she had time. When [John] knocked on the door, [his] aunt and uncle met him with big smiles on [their] faces. [They] had already talked to John's [parents]. [Aunt Tina] hugged [John] and said she would drive [him] to school. Aunt Tina made John promise to get up on time tomorrow. Then [she] grabbed [her] keys and drove John to school.

"Kids Did It!"   National Geographic Kids   Helen
– Wiley Dotzenroth in a shark cage
– Fifteen 10- to 14-year-old kids to South Africa on 2007 National Geographic Kids Expedition
– All won a National Geographic Kids photo and essay competition
– Saw great white sharks, cape fur seals, southern right whales, and penguins
– Helped some hurt penguins
– Team rode around in Land Rovers. Saw elephants, rhinos, African buffaloes, lions, and leopards
– Team raised $10,000 before trip to help a school in South Africa get computer and Internet access

---

"Kids Did It!" National Geographic Kids   Helen

Fifteen kids who won a National Geographic photo and essay contest went on an expedition to South Africa. They saw lots of animals, including great white sharks, Cape fur seals, southern right whales, and injured penguins. They also rode in Land Rovers and saw elephants, rhinos, African buffalo, lions, and leopards. The team raised money to get a computer and Internet access for a school.

Helen

"Kids Did It!"
National Geographic Kids

Fifteen kids went on a South African expedition because they won a National Geographic contest. They saw many animals, including great white sharks, whales, elephants, and lions. The children also raised money to help a school get on the Internet.

Perfect Pair

Root words

Materials:
student copies of the sock pattern on page 88
list of Greek or Latin roots (see below)
scissors
colored pencils

A student chooses a root from the list. He adds a prefix and/or a suffix to the root and writes the resulting word on a sock cutout. Next, he adds a different prefix and/or suffix to the same root and writes the new word on a second sock cutout. Then he underlines the root in each word and lightly colors each cutout. He repeats the process to form two additional words to write on his two remaining cutouts.

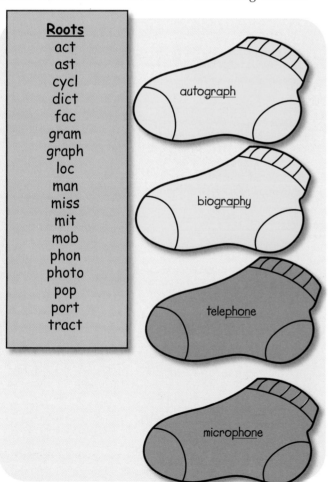

Roots
act
ast
cycl
dict
fac
gram
graph
loc
man
miss
mit
mob
phon
photo
pop
port
tract

autograph

biography

telephone

microphone

Recommended Reading

Comprehension

Materials:
large plastic resealable bag
index cards (one per student)
clothespins (one per student)

After a student reads a book, she lists on a card the book's title and author. She writes a review of the book in a brief paragraph. Then, she slides the book and card inside a plastic bag and clips it to a line attached to a board titled "Recommended Reading."

Love That Dog!

Love That Dog by Sharon Creech is one of the best books I have ever read! The story is written as a journal of poems. Each poem is easy to read and tells a lot about Jack, the main character. This book has a surprise ending that makes it even better! Read this book!

Alisha

Small, Smaller, Smallest

Adjectives

Materials:
newspapers, magazines, or old books
list of adjectives
lined paper
scissors
glue

A student chooses an adjective from the list and records it on his paper along with the word's comparative and superlative forms. Next, he cuts out pictures that match the descriptive words and glues the pictures to his paper. Then he uses each term in a descriptive sentence about the matching picture.

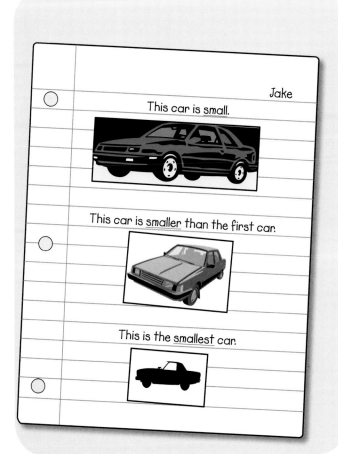

File It Under *Alternative*

Synonyms

Materials:
file folders, each labeled with an overused word as shown
thesaurus
paper

A student chooses a file folder, finds in the thesaurus the word on the folder's tab, and then lists synonyms for the word inside the folder. Next, the child writes a short story based on the overused word. For example, for the word *good,* a student could title her work "The Good Story." Then, throughout the story, she would describe events that fit the title without using the word *good.* When she's finished, she places her story in the corresponding folder.

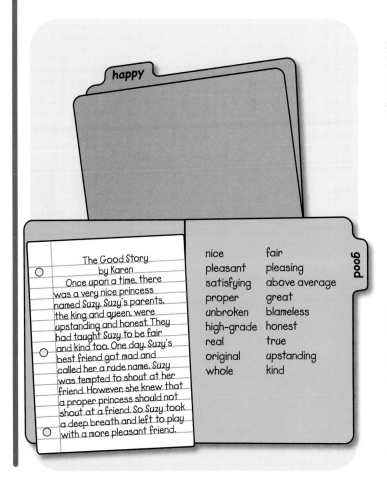

Sort It!

Using a dictionary

Materials:
student copies of the word cards on page 88
paper
dictionary
scissors
glue

A student folds and then unfolds a sheet of paper to create four sections and titles each section as shown. Next, he cuts apart the word cards and arranges them in alphabetical order. He looks up each word and reads its definition. Then he sorts the words into categories and glues each card in place.

Eat		Feel	Weston
abalone	bonbon	astonishment	bedraggled
legume	fillet	belligerent	desolate
pemmican	russet	hysterical	optimistic

Do		Use	
admonish	ascend	antiseptic	bicuspid
bestow	cackle	contraption	hyperbole
excavate	mesmerize	ocarina	windlass

Quiz Me!

Nonfiction text features

For partners

Materials:
2 copies of the same grade-level textbook
index cards (five cards per student)

Each student skims the book's table of contents, glossary, and index. Then she writes on separate index cards five questions her partner can answer by studying the book's text features. She writes each answer on the back of the card. When each child is finished, the partners trade cards. Each student uses the book to answer each question and then flips the card over to check his work.

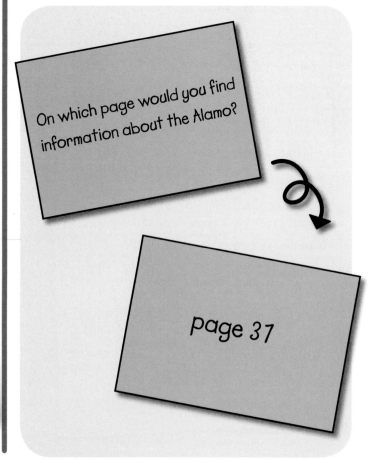

On which page would you find information about the Alamo?

page 37

On the Web

Pronouns

Materials:
recently read story
paper

A student creates on his paper a pronoun web that includes all the subject, object, and/or possessive pronouns. Next, he rereads the story. When the child reads a pronoun, he identifies the noun it replaces and adds a bubble for that noun next to the corresponding pronoun on his web. (If a pronoun is repeatedly used to refer to the same noun, the student just lists the noun once.) The student continues to expand his web in this manner as time allows.

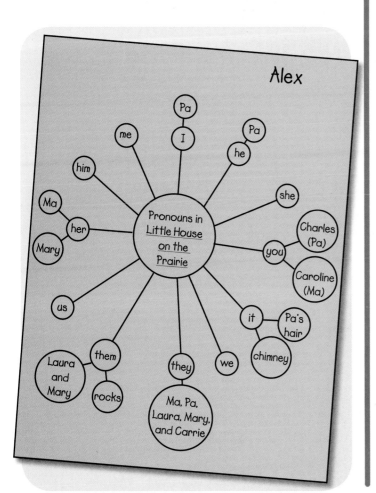

Revising the Retell

Point of view

Materials:
picture books
binder titled "Another Side of the Story"
paper

A student reads a book. Then she chooses one of the story's minor characters and rewrites the story from that character's point of view. She adds her finished story to the class's collection in the binder.

A River Run

Guide words

Materials:
student copies of page 89 labeled with two guide words
spelling or vocabulary list
scissors
glue

A student writes each spelling or vocabulary word on a different raft, cuts out the rafts, and arranges the words in alphabetical order. Next, the child decides which words are listed before, between, and after the guide words. Then he glues each word to the page to show his work.

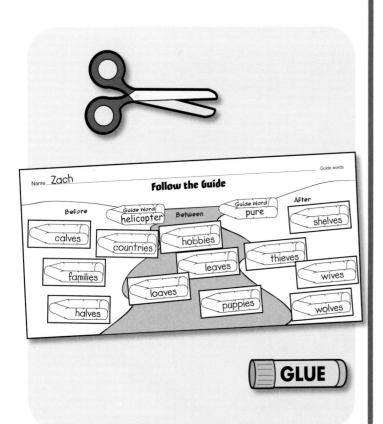

Facts Wanted

Fact and opinion

Materials:
classified ads
paper

A student chooses an advertisement and labels her paper with three columns as shown. The child then lists the advertised item, evaluates the ad's statements, and records information about the ad in the appropriate columns. She repeats the steps with additional ads as time allows.

Item	Fact	Opinion
Bichon Frise	AKC female pup shots/dewormed	Adorable
Blue Tick Beagle	AKC reg. DOB Sept. 07 2M/2F	Great pets or hunting dogs
Brittany Spaniel	2 yrs. old	Excellent pet
Chihuahuas	CKC reg. Teacup dewormed 1st shots 9 weeks old	Good house dog

Comic Talk

Dialogue

Materials:
comic strips, cut apart
paper

A student chooses a comic strip and lists on his paper the strip's main characters. Then he writes a story retelling the comic's events. As the child writes the story, he punctuates the text from each speech bubble as dialogue, adding commas and quotation marks as necessary.

"Peanuts" Dialogue   Trevor
Main characters: Lucy and Linus

Lucy leans over to look at something on the ground.

As she looks, she announces, "Well, look here! A big yellow butterfly!"

Then Linus catches up to Lucy.

Lucy uses her know-it-all voice to explain why there is a butterfly there.

She states, "It's unusual to see one this time of year unless, of course, he flew up from Brazil...I'll bet that's it!"

Lucy squats down and says, "They do that sometimes you know... They fly up from Brazil, and they..."

Linus bends over and studies the object on the ground.

"This is no butterfly," he tells her. "This is a potato chip!"

Lucy refuses to be wrong about anything, so she looks closer at the chip and declares, "Well, I'll be! So it is! I wonder how a potato chip got all the way up here from Brazil?"

Build It!

Parts of speech

Materials:
5 resealable plastic bags, each containing word
    cards from a specific part of speech
colored pencils or markers
paper

A student draws a card from each group. She uses the cards to create a sentence. Next, she records the sentence on her paper, writing each noun, verb, adjective, adverb, and prepositional phrase in a different color according to the code. She then returns the cards to their respective sets, draws new words, and continues the activity in the same manner as time allows.

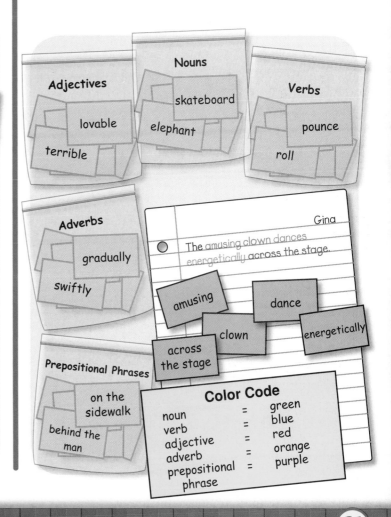

Spelling Practice

Commonly misspelled words

Materials:
copy of the bananas from page 90, cut out
    and fastened with a brad as shown
dictionary
paper

A student reads the list of words on the first banana and identifies each misspelled word, using the dictionary as necessary. The child then writes on his paper the correct spelling of each misspelled word. He repeats the process with each remaining banana as time allows.

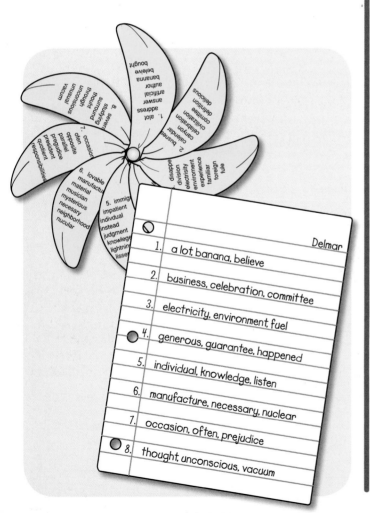

Delmar

1. a lot, banana, believe
2. business, celebration, committee
3. electricity, environment, fuel
4. generous, guarantee, happened
5. individual, knowledge, listen
6. manufacture, necessary, nuclear
7. occasion, often, prejudice
8. thought, unconscious, vacuum

One Book to Another

Compare and contrast

Materials:
several picture books on similar topics
paper

A student chooses two books and reads each one. Next, the child draws a Venn diagram on her paper. She labels each circle with a book's title and then compares the books.

Madeline

Two Bad Ants
about insects

The ants look like real ants.

The ants get into a lot of trouble.

The ants don't know what anything in the human world is.

written as a story

The ants learn a lesson.

about bugs

picture books

The bugs act and talk like humans.

Both kinds of bugs live in the human world with big human things.

Diary of a Spider
about spiders

The spider goes to school.

The spiders have hats and bows that make them seem like people.

Spider's best friend is a worm.

written as diary entries with funny pictures

Mix It Up

Compound sentences

Materials:
copy of the sentence strips on page 91,
   cut apart and placed in a bag
paper

   A student draws two strips from the bag. He reads the sentences and decides which conjunction he should use to combine the two sentences. The child records the compound sentence on his paper, adding the appropriate punctuation, and returns the strips to the bag. He then shakes the bag and repeats the process. He continues in this manner as time allows.

Alan

I need to finish reading this book, but I can hardly wait to see the new movie.

I can hardly wait to see the new movie.

I need to finish reading this book.

Super Sale

Paragraphs

Materials:
classified ads for cars and trucks
list of abbreviations for common auto terms,
   like the one shown
paper

   A student chooses an advertisement and reads it to identify the car's features, using the list of abbreviations for help as needed. Then the child writes a paragraph describing the car in its most positive light. As time allows, the child illustrates the paragraph.

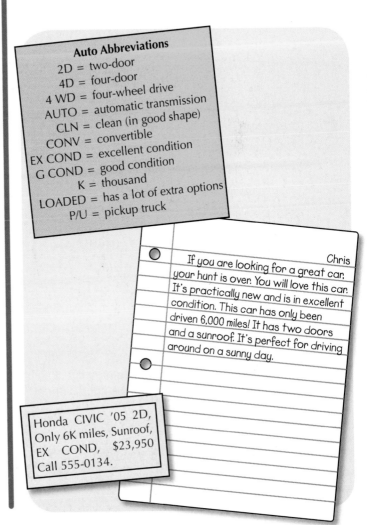

Auto Abbreviations
2D = two-door
4D = four-door
4 WD = four-wheel drive
AUTO = automatic transmission
CLN = clean (in good shape)
CONV = convertible
EX COND = excellent condition
G COND = good condition
K = thousand
LOADED = has a lot of extra options
P/U = pickup truck

Chris
If you are looking for a great car, your hunt is over. You will love this car. It's practically new and is in excellent condition. This car has only been driven 6,000 miles! It has two doors and a sunroof. It's perfect for driving around on a sunny day.

Honda CIVIC '05 2D,
Only 6K miles, Sunroof,
EX COND, $23,950
Call 555-0134.

Spiced Up!

Idioms

Materials:
copy of the idiom cards from page 91, cut apart
paper

A student selects a card. He writes on his paper a descriptive sentence that includes the selected idiom. He also writes a sentence that explains the idiom. Then he selects another card. He continues writing sentences in this manner as time allows or until all the cards have been used.

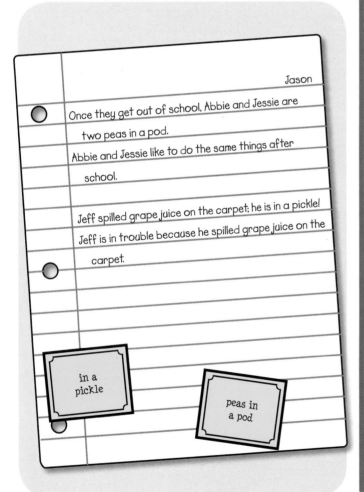

Jason

Once they get out of school, Abbie and Jessie are two peas in a pod.
Abbie and Jessie like to do the same things after school.

Jeff spilled grape juice on the carpet; he is in a pickle!
Jeff is in trouble because he spilled grape juice on the carpet.

in a pickle

peas in a pod

Random Reporting

Comprehension

Materials:
recently read chapter book
2 dice
code like the one shown
paper

A student rolls the dice, adds the numbers rolled, and turns to that chapter in the book. Then the child rolls the dice again, adds the numbers, and identifies the matching letter in the code. Next, she reviews the chapter and lists on her paper words from the chapter that begin with the corresponding letter. Finally, the child describes the chapter, its setting, the main character, or an event from the chapter using words that begin with the assigned letter. She then counts the number of words she used and writes and circles the number at the top of her paper.

Sum		Letter
2	=	a
3	=	b
4	=	c
5	=	d
6	=	f
7	=	m
8	=	o
9	=	r
10	=	s
11	=	t
12	=	w

(9)   Sarah

Hatchet, Chapter 10
Letter: b
Words: brightening, burned, brought, broke, began, Brian, banked, been, base, breaking, but, being, back, burning, build, be, bed, blowing, blaze, before

Brian builds a bright fire. He breaks branches and limbs. Burning the dry wood makes Brian feel better. He banks the fire to keep it burning when he goes out to get more wood. Brian brings back more wood and realizes he can use a burning stick to build a signal fire.

Hatchet
by Gary Paulsen

Alphabetic Action

Verbs

Materials:
paper (four sheets per student)
dictionary
scissors
stapler

A student cuts four sheets of paper in half, stacks and folds the half sheets, and staples them along the fold to make a booklet. Next, he labels the booklet's pages with the letters of the alphabet, skipping *X.* Then the child brainstorms action verbs that begin with each letter, using a dictionary as necessary. He lists each verb and draws a simple sketch that illustrates the action. Then he decorates the cover and keeps the booklet as a handy writing resource.

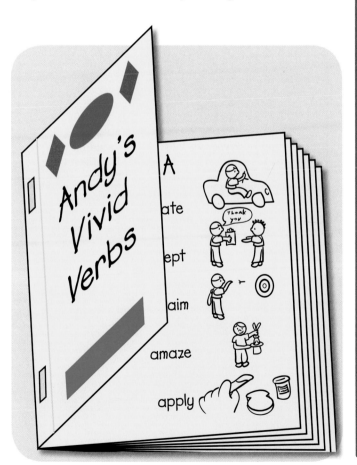

Out of the Box

Descriptions

Materials:
box of common classroom items
envelopes (at least one per student)
index cards (at least two cards per student)
paper

Possible items include a crayon, a pencil, a marker, a pad of sticky notes, a calculator, a ruler, and a protractor.

A student chooses an object from the box. On her paper, she describes the object from the object's point of view without naming the object. She writes her final draft on one index card and draws the object on another index card. She places both cards in an envelope. Then she repeats the steps with other objects as time allows. To use the completed cards, a pair of students shuffle their cards and place them facedown. The partners take turns turning over two cards and looking for a match, each student trying to collect more pairs.

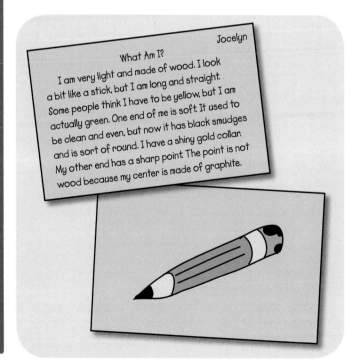

All About Me

Idioms

Materials:
copy of the list of idioms from page 92
paper

A student writes his initials vertically on his paper. Beside each letter, he writes words that begin with that letter and that describe himself. Next, he chooses three idioms from the list. He then uses each selected idiom in a descriptive sentence about himself, incorporating into each sentence at least one word from his descriptive list. Finally, he underlines the idioms and circles the descriptive words he used in his sentences.

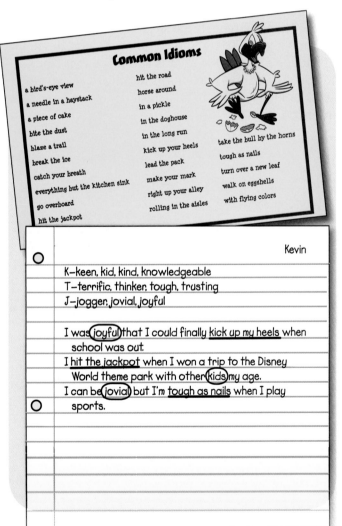

Common Idioms

a bird's-eye view
a needle in a haystack
a piece of cake
bite the dust
blaze a trail
break the ice
catch your breath
everything but the kitchen sink
go overboard
hit the jackpot

hit the road
horse around
in a pickle
in the doghouse
in the long run
kick up your heels
lead the pack
make your mark
right up your alley
rolling in the aisles

take the bull by the horns
tough as nails
turn over a new leaf
walk on eggshells
with flying colors

Kevin

K–keen, kid, kind, knowledgeable
T–terrific, thinker, tough, trusting
J–jogger, jovial, joyful

I was joyful that I could finally kick up my heels when school was out.
I hit the jackpot when I won a trip to the Disney World theme park with other kids my age.
I can be jovial but I'm tough as nails when I play sports.

Capture It!

Main idea

Materials:
unillustrated book of poetry
colored pencils
drawing paper

A student selects a poem to read. Next, she closes her eyes, visualizes the poem's main idea, and illustrates it on her paper. She then writes on her drawing the poem's title, author, and main idea.

Jessie
"Weather"–Anonymous

The main idea of this poem is that no matter what the weather is like outside, people just have to deal with it the best they can.

Poetry

Piecing It Together

Compound sentences

Materials:
4 resealable plastic bags, each containing
    a set of word cards from page 93
paper

A student selects a bag, arranges the word cards inside to form a compound sentence, and then writes the sentence on his paper. He returns the cards to the bag and then repeats the process with the remaining bags as time allows.

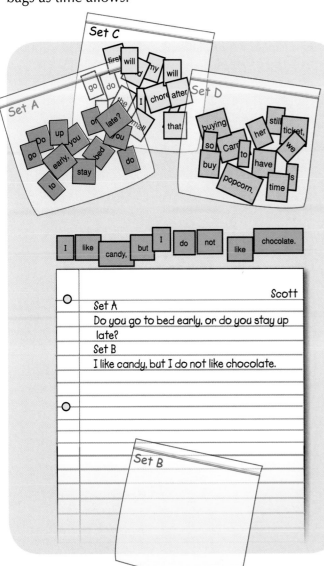

Scott

Set A
Do you go to bed early, or do you stay up late?
Set B
I like candy, but I do not like chocolate.

Tell Me How

Expository writing

Materials:
drawing paper
crayons or colored pencils

A student writes on her paper several steps that explain how to complete a center activity currently being used in the classroom. She adds helpful illustrations to some of the steps.

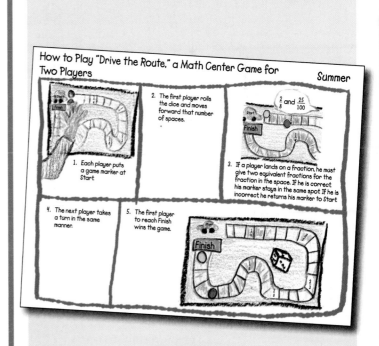

How to Play "Drive the Route," a Math Center Game for Two Players   Summer

1. Each player puts a game marker at Start

2. The first player rolls the dice and moves forward that number of spaces.

3. If a player lands on a fraction, he must give two equivalent fractions for the fraction in the space. If he is correct his marker stays in the same spot. If he is incorrect he returns his marker to Start

4. The next player takes a turn in the same manner.

5. The first player to reach Finish wins the game.

I Mean It!

Multiple-meaning words

Materials:
copy of the multiple-meaning word list from page 92
drawing paper (one sheet per student)
colored pencils

A student selects a word from the list. Across the top of his paper, he writes a sentence in which his selected word has two different meanings. He illustrates the sentence in the remaining space.

Multiple-Meaning Words				
ball	date	kind	point	sink
bank	drop	light	present	star
bark	face	like	press	stick
bat	fair	line	rare	story
bend	fan	mean	ring	tire
bill	file	mine	roll	trip
bowl	fly	miss	rose	vault
can	grave	order	run	watch
case	hide	pen	second	well
check	jam	play	ship	yard

The jar of jam caused a traffic jam.

Picture Perfect

Cause and effect

Materials:
magazines, newspapers, or picture calendars
construction paper (one sheet per student)
scissors
glue
markers

A student cuts out a picture from the provided materials and glues it to the center of her paper. Above the picture, she writes a statement about what is happening in the picture. Below the picture, she writes an effect of her statement. Then the student turns her paper over, selects a second picture, and repeats the process.

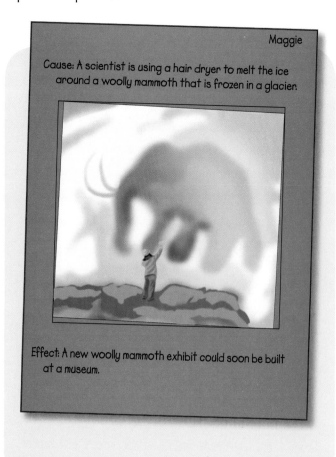

Maggie

Cause: A scientist is using a hair dryer to melt the ice around a woolly mammoth that is frozen in a glacier.

Effect: A new woolly mammoth exhibit could soon be built at a museum.

All Sorts of Fun!

Nouns

Materials:
sheet of construction paper labeled with
   the diagram shown
index cards labeled with the words in the box

A student sorts the word cards onto the mat's "Noun" or "Not a Noun" boxes. Next, he sorts the nouns onto the mat's "Singular" and "Plural" boxes. Finally, he sorts the singular nouns and the plural nouns onto their respective "Common" and "Proper" boxes.

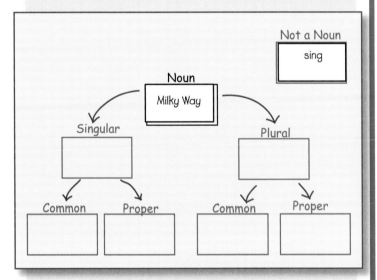

Words to Sort

Americans	geese	nurses	submarine
Baltimore	Jessica	Ohio	New Orleans
children	jump	pencil	Kennedys
Christmases	libraries	piano	very
colorful	Milky Way	sing	weather

Staying in Touch

Friendly letter

Materials:
construction paper (one sheet per student)
scissors
glue
paper

A student writes on her paper a friendly letter to a friend or relative, making sure she includes the letter's five main parts. She then cuts a flap for each part as shown. Next, the student glues her letter to a sheet of construction paper, being careful not to glue the flaps down. Then she lifts each flap, in turn, and writes the name of the corresponding letter part.

Highlight of the Day

Prefixes and suffixes

Materials:
student copies of the passage on page 93
2 highlighters (pink and blue)

A student reads his copy of the passage. As he reads, he highlights all the prefixes in pink and all the suffixes in blue.

Name Alex

Prefixes and suffixes

Oh, Brother!

Brothers can be such pests! Take my brother, for instance. His side of our room is **un**believ**ably** mess**y**. He never picks up his things. His side of the floor is so **un**kempt that he cannot even see his feet once he sets them on the floor. His belong**ings** have a way of creeping into my neat and tidy side of the room. Plus, any time something of his **dis**appears, he tries to blame it on me.

"I'm not the one who lives like a pig!" I always say.

Well, I have decid**ed** to teach my brother a lesson. Tonight, after he falls asleep, I am going to pile all his stuff into his closet. (The amount will like**ly** reach the ceiling.) Then, when he wakes up in the morning and opens his closet door, an avalanche of cloth**ing**, sports equip**ment**, and video games will fall on him. That ought to teach him not to leave his possess**ions** lying around, don't you think?

Color Code
pink = prefix
blue = suffix

What's Cooking?

Using an index

Materials:
cookbooks
index cards (one per student)

A student finds her favorite food ingredient in the index of a cookbook. She copies as many recipe entries for that ingredient as she can onto the front of an index card. Next, she looks up each listed recipe and selects the one that most appeals to her. She then records that recipe's name on the back of her index card, along with an explanation of how the index helped her find it.

Recipes That Contain Chocolate		Jenny
Chocoberry Shake	36	
Chocolate Apples	134	
Chocolate Chip Cookies	208	
Chocolate-Lace Pie	101	
Chocolate Marshmallows	105	
Chocolate Noodles	109	
Chocolate Quicksand	122	
Chocolate Sparkle	98	
Chocolate Wafers	210	

Recipe I selected: Chocolate Quicksand

The index helped me rule out any recipes that did not contain my favorite ingredient. It also kept me from having to look through the entire book to find a recipe I'd like to try.

Tasty Treats

Verb tenses

Materials:
6 index cards labeled as shown
paper

A student divides a sheet of paper into three columns and labels them as shown. Next, he selects an index card and reads the verb. He uses the appropriate tense of the verb to write a sentence in each column of his paper. He repeats the process with each remaining card.

Past	Present	Future
The popcorn popped in the microwave.	He pops pieces of popcorn into his mouth one after another.	We will pop popcorn for the party.

sizzle

fizz

pop

slurp

gulp

crunch

Take Your Turn

Persuasive writing

Materials:
paper

A student writes a paragraph attempting to convince her teacher that she should be allowed to teach a lesson to the class. She decides which topic she would like to teach and the day on which she would like to teach it. As she writes, the student includes reasons why her teacher should grant her request.

Brandy

I love to study history, especially the Civil War. I have been interested in anything to do with the Civil War since I was little. I have read a lot of Civil War books. I have also seen every movie I could that has been made about the Civil War. My parents even take me to the museum as often as they can so I can learn more about that time period. Both my parents and my grandparents are helping me collect pictures for the Civil War album I am working on. Because I know so much about this topic, I think I should be allowed to teach a lesson about it. I would like to teach the lesson on Wednesday, since you said last week that that is the day we would start to learn about the Civil War. I think my classmates would enjoy hearing me tell about the war and seeing my collection of Civil War items.

Cartoon Caper

Sequencing

Materials:
drawing paper
colored pencils
stapler

A student recalls a major event from the beginning, the middle, and the end of a favorite cartoon, book, or movie. Next, she folds and then unfolds her paper to create four equal sections and cuts the sections apart. The student decorates one page like the cover of a comic book and numbers the other pages. She then uses illustrations and captions to retell each main event in order. When she's finished, she staples the pages together.

Colorful Boxes

Irregular verbs

For partners

Materials:
copies of page 94, one per student pair
2 colored pencils of different colors
scissors

A student cuts apart the gameboards and answer key from a copy of page 94 and places the answer key facedown. He selects a board and places it between himself and his partner. Next, he selects a box and uses a colored pencil to record in it both the past tense and past participle forms of that verb. His partner then takes a turn in the same manner using a different colored pencil. Once all the boxes are used, the duo checks the answers with the key. The students color each correct box in its corresponding color. The player with more colored boxes wins. The partners then select a different gameboard and play again as time allows.

Board A

1. am	2. begin	3. eat	4. forgive forgave forgiven
5. is	6. leave	7. read read read	8. shake
9. sing sang sung	10. slide	11. swim	12. teach taught taught
13. hear	14. shrink	15. write	16. catch

Make It Personal

Prepositional phrases

Materials:
drawing paper (one sheet per student)
colored pencils
markers

A student uses colored pencils to draw a picture of himself doing something he likes to do. In the drawing he includes several objects in different locations. He then uses the markers to write on his drawing prepositional phrases telling the location of the objects.

over my head
in my hand
around my neck
by my belt
on the trail
with my dog

A Handshake

Descriptive writing

Materials:
poster board hand cutout labeled with the story starter shown
scrap paper
paper

A student copies the story starter onto her paper. Next, she brainstorms on scrap paper vivid words, phrases, and examples of figurative language that could help her describe the handshake in detail and tell how long it lasted, how it made the character feel, and what happened to the character afterward. The student then uses her brainstormed list to help her finish the story.

Dylan was perfect. Teachers liked him because he made great grades. Students liked him because he was a great friend and good at sports. Then one day, his life changed forever. It all started with a handshake...

strong, firm grip like a linebacker for the Pittsburgh Steelers

handshake's up-and-down motion almost took off his arm

squeezed his fingers together so hard he wanted to cry like a baby

hand so bruised he couldn't write anymore, grip a ball, or pat a friend on the back

Similar Sayings

Thesaurus

Materials:
copy of the idioms on page 92
thesaurus
paper

A student chooses an idiom. He uses the thesaurus to find synonyms for words in the idiom. Next, on his paper, the student rewrites the idiom using synonyms and then lists the original idiom along with two other sayings in a multiple-choice format. The child repeats the process as time allows to create a quiz. Finally, each student trades his paper with a partner and takes her synonym quiz.

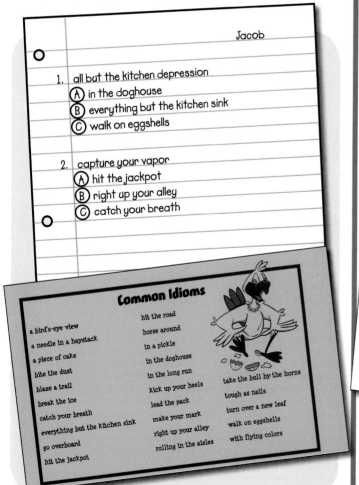

Jacob

1. all but the kitchen depression
   (A) in the doghouse
   (B) everything but the kitchen sink
   (C) walk on eggshells

2. capture your vapor
   (A) hit the jackpot
   (B) right up your alley
   (C) catch your breath

Common Idioms

a bird's-eye view
a needle in a haystack
a piece of cake
bite the dust
blaze a trail
break the ice
catch your breath
everything but the kitchen sink
go overboard
hit the jackpot

hit the road
horse around
in a pickle
in the doghouse
in the long run
kick up your heels
lead the pack
make your mark
right up your alley
rolling in the aisles

take the bull by the horns
tough as nails
turn over a new leaf
walk on eggshells
with flying colors

Now Reporting

Important details

Materials:
student copies of page 95
newspaper articles

A student chooses and reads an article. Next, she reviews the article as she fills in a copy of page 95. Then she uses her notes to summarize the article.

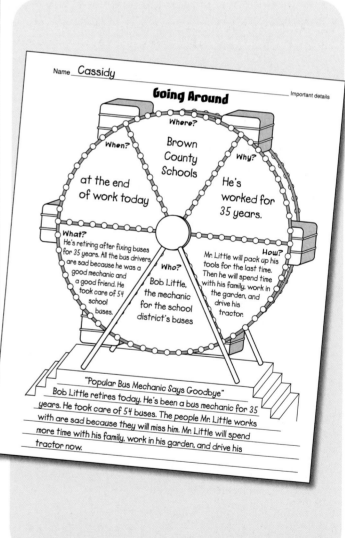

Name Cassidy

Important details

Going Around

Where? Brown County Schools

When? at the end of work today

Why? He's worked for 35 years.

What? He's retiring after fixing buses for 35 years. All the bus drivers are sad because he was a good mechanic and a good friend. He took care of 54 school buses.

How? Mr. Little will pack up his tools for the last time. Then he will spend time with his family, work in the garden, and drive his tractor.

Who? Bob Little, the mechanic for the school district's buses

"Popular Bus Mechanic Says Goodbye"
Bob Little retires today. He's been a bus mechanic for 35 years. He took care of 54 buses. The people Mr. Little works with are sad because they will miss him. Mr. Little will spend more time with his family, work in his garden, and drive his tractor now.

Verb Hunt

Verb tenses

Materials:
newspaper sports pages
markers
paper

A student finds and circles at least ten verbs on a sports page. Next, the child draws and labels a three-column chart as shown. He identifies the tense of each circled verb and writes it in the correct chart column. Then he adds each verb's other two tenses. The student continues in this manner until his chart includes all three tenses for each circled word on the newspaper page.

In the News

Summarizing

Materials:
newspapers or magazines
science or social studies textbook
construction paper (one sheet per student)
scissors
glue

A student reads a chapter from a current unit of study. She identifies the chapter's main idea and most important details and then drafts a one- or two-sentence summary. Next, the student cuts from a newspaper or magazine the words she needs for her summary and glues them on her paper, as shown, writing in any words she could not find.

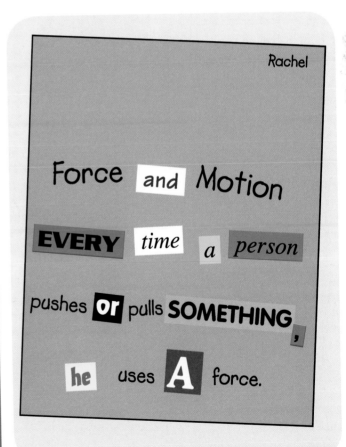

Same or Opposite?

Synonyms and antonyms

Materials:
student copies of the synonym and antonym
   strips from page 96, cut apart
list of words that have both antonyms and synonyms shown
thesaurus
paper bag

   A student chooses a word from the list and writes it on a strip where indicated. Next, the child adds a synonym and an antonym for the word on the appropriate lines. He then folds the strip to hide the word, as shown, and drops the strip into the bag. He repeats the steps as time allows. Later, students in a pair take turns drawing strips, reading the listed synonyms and antonyms, and guessing the hidden words.

Word List	
accept	part
allow	real
collect	respect
easy	rise
enter	seek
flexible	show
kind	strong
knowledge	support
move	teach
native	tight
new	true
open	wide

Comic Relief

Predictions

Materials:
comic strips with 3 or 4 panels, each with
   the final panel removed and taped to the back side
paper

   A child chooses a comic strip. On her paper, she summarizes the first two or three panels. Next, she records a prediction about the final panel. Then she flips the strip over, reads the final panel, and compares it with her prediction.

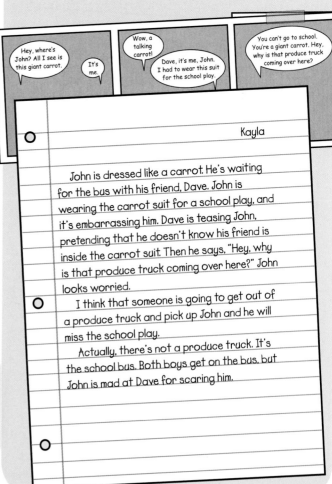

Super Sentences

Complex sentences

Materials:
construction paper strips of different colors
list of subordinating conjunctions shown
glue
paper

A student takes two different-colored strips and writes a related sentence on each strip. He glues the strips to his paper and then combines the sentences, using a subordinating conjunction to create a complex sentence. He repeats the steps as time allows or until he has written three different complex sentences.

Subordinating Conjunctions	
after	so
although	that
as if	though
because	unless
before	until
if	when
in order that	where
since	while

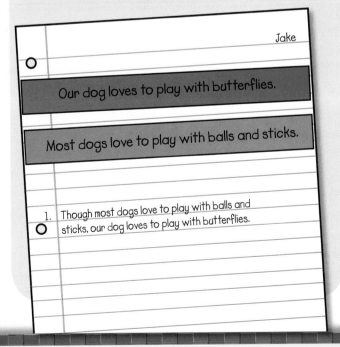

Jake

Our dog loves to play with butterflies.

Most dogs love to play with balls and sticks.

1. Though most dogs love to play with balls and sticks, our dog loves to play with butterflies.

Roll and Write

Narrative writing

Materials:
copy of the sequence code from page 96, cut out
copy of the sentence strips from page 96, cut apart
die
paper

A student rolls the die and takes the same-numbered strip. She rolls the die again and checks the sequence code. Then the child writes a story using the sentence as part of her story's beginning, middle, or end according to the code.

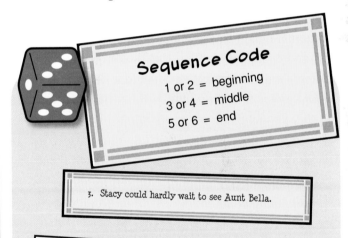

Sequence Code
1 or 2 = beginning
3 or 4 = middle
5 or 6 = end

3. Stacy could hardly wait to see Aunt Bella.

Someone New   Anita

Stacy heard her mother talking into her cell phone. Her mom said, "Bella, I don't think you'll even recognize Stacy. The last time you saw her, she was only two years old."

Stacy felt as though she knew Aunt Bella even though she had been living in Africa for ten years. Her mom's phone call might mean that her aunt was coming to visit. Stacy could hardly wait to see Aunt Bella.

Stacy ran around the corner. She waited until she saw her mom close her phone. Then she asked, "Who was that, Mom?"

Stacy's mom looked at her with a big grin and said, "That was Aunt Bella. She's coming home! She'll be here next week." Stacy hugged her mom. She had waited almost her whole life to hug her Aunt Bella. Soon she'd get to do it!

Definition Teller

Vocabulary

For partners

Materials:
8" paper squares (one per student)
list of 8 vocabulary words
glossary or dictionary

To make a teller, a student folds his square's opposite corners together and then unfolds the paper. He folds each corner to the center crease. Next, the child flips the paper over and folds each corner to the center. The student flips the paper over again and numbers each triangle as shown. Then he turns the paper over and writes a vocabulary word on each small triangle. He unfolds each large triangle and writes the matching definition under each triangle. To play, the student and a partner take turns picking a number, opening and closing a teller that number of times, and then picking a word and checking its definition.

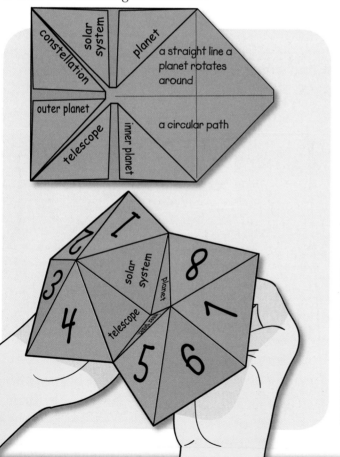

In the Picture

Fact and opinion

Materials:
magazine, newspaper, or calendar pictures
paper

A student chooses a picture. She draws a T chart on her paper, labeling each column as shown. Next, the child writes at least five facts and five opinions about the picture. Then she staples the picture to her paper. She repeats the steps with another picture as time allows.

Facts	Opinions
This man is eating a cheeseburger.	The lettuce is pretty fresh.
The cheeseburger has at least two tomato slices.	The cheeseburger is delicious.
The man is wearing a purple colored sweater.	The man's hair is too short.
The bun is covered in sesame seeds.	There are too many tomato slices on the cheeseburger.
The man is outside.	There is not enough cheese on the burger.

Elena

A Little Assistance

Helping verbs

Materials:
large index cards, each programmed with a different helping verb
highlighter

A student chooses a card, flips it over, and writes a sentence on the back of the card using that card's helping verb. Next, he highlights the helping verb and main verb in his sentence and records his initials at the end of the sentence. Then he repeats the process with other cards, writing sentences with other helping verbs as time allows.

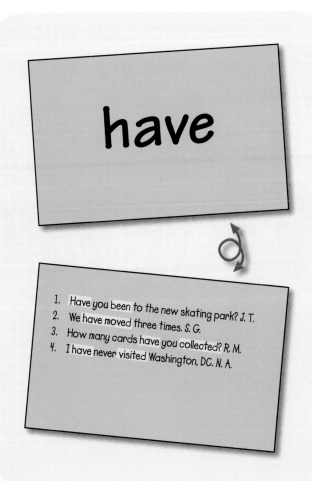

have

1. Have you been to the new skating park? J. T.
2. We have moved three times. S. G.
3. How many cards have you collected? R. M.
4. I have never visited Washington, DC. N. A.

Here We Go!

Note taking

Materials:
student copies of page 95
grade-appropriate magazine articles
sticky note (six per student)

A student labels six sticky notes with the questions shown. Next, she reads an article. As she reads, she places each sticky note beside text in the article that answers the question on the note. After reading, the child reviews the placement of the sticky notes, adjusts them as necessary, and jots an important word or phrase on each note. Next, the student transfers each sticky note to her copy of page 95 and adds relevant notes to each section. Then she summarizes her notes at the bottom of the page.

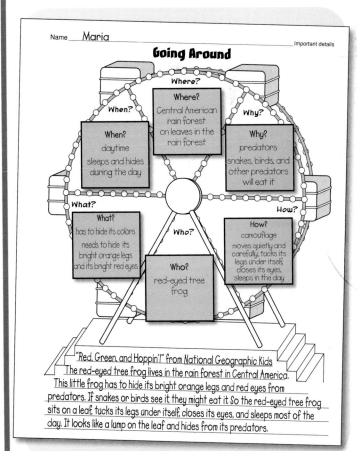

Name **Maria** Important details

Going Around

Where?
Central American rain forest on leaves in the rain forest

When?
daytime sleeps and hides during the day

Why?
predators snakes, birds, and other predators will eat it

What?
has to hide its colors needs to hide its bright orange legs and its bright red eyes

Who?
red-eyed tree frog

How?
camouflage moves quietly and carefully, tucks its legs under itself, closes its eyes, sleeps in the day

"Red, Green, and Hoppin'!" from National Geographic Kids
The red-eyed tree frog lives in the rain forest in Central America. This little frog has to hide its bright orange legs and red eyes from predators. If snakes or birds see it, they might eat it. So the red-eyed tree frog sits on a leaf, tucks its legs under itself, closes its eyes, and sleeps most of the day. It looks like a lump on the leaf and hides from its predators.

Hands-On Comparisons

Analogies

Materials:
container of assorted objects
paper

Possible objects include a pebble, a pen, a pencil, chalk, a shell, a ruler, a protractor, and a twig.

A student chooses two or more objects and creates an analogy to compare them. He records the analogy on his paper. Next, he adds a sentence that explains his analogy and then returns the items to the container. He continues creating different analogies in this manner as time allows.

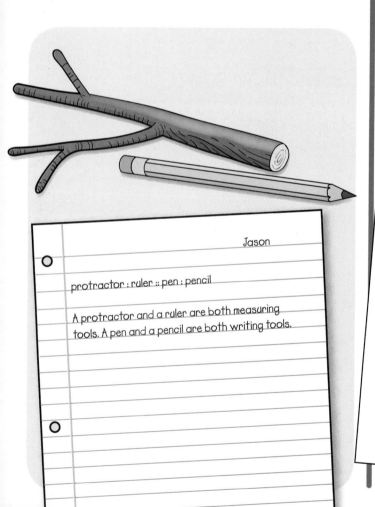

Jason

protractor : ruler :: pen : pencil

A protractor and a ruler are both measuring tools. A pen and a pencil are both writing tools.

Graphic Recap

Retelling

Materials:
student copies of page 97
crayons or colored pencils

A student draws a picture in each panel to share the most important ideas and details of a fiction or nonfiction reading assignment.

Name Olivia

Graphic Recap   Retelling

Use words and pictures to show the important ideas from your reading.

Title:
The Great Kapok Tree

This is my home.

We pollinate the plants.

We have seen people chop down trees and burn the underbrush.

This tree is home for many animals and birds.

Please don't chop down this tree.

Poetic Phrases

Prepositions

Materials:
index cards (six per student)
list of common prepositions
hole puncher
yarn

A student chooses a preposition and thinks of a noun that begins with the same letter. He records the alliterative phrase on an index card and illustrates it on the back of the card, using an arrow to show the preposition's meaning. He repeats the process with five more prepositions. Then the student punches a hole in the top and bottom edge of each card, ties the cards together with yarn, and hangs his mobile to display it.

under the
umbrella

Community Outreach

Business letters

Materials:
names and addresses of local businesses
business envelope (one per student)
paper

A student chooses a business. She writes a letter to the company asking questions about the business, such as how long it has been part of the community, what services it provides, and what types of education and skills its employees must have. Then the child addresses an envelope, folds her letter in thirds, and slips it in the envelope so it can be mailed.

1026 Market Street
Greensboro, NC 99999
February 14, 2008

Pets 'n' More Photography
3278 Main Street
Greensboro, NC 99999

To Whom It May Concern:

I am a student at High Grove Elementary. My school bus goes by your store every day. I would like to learn more about your business.
How long has your store been open?
Do you take pictures of people at your store?
Do you take pictures of people or things anywhere else in town?
If I wanted to work at your store, what would I have to know?
Thank you for taking the time to answer my questions. I look forward to hearing from you.

Sincerely,
Shannon Taylor

High Grove Elementary
1026 Market Street
Greensboro, NC 99999

Pets 'n' More Photography
3278 Main Street
Greensboro, NC 99999

Just Joking Around

Homophones

Materials:
copy of the homophone list on page 98
drawing paper (one sheet per student)
colored pencils

A student selects a homophone pair from the list. Next, he writes on his paper a simple joke using the homophone pair. Then he illustrates his joke.

Why did the old lady put running shoes on a fly?

So she could yell, "Shoo, fly!"

Colored Contrasts

Character comparisons

Materials:
construction paper (one sheet per student)
construction paper squares: green, blue, and yellow
   (one of each color per student)
glue
markers

A student programs a blue square with the name of the main character from a recently read story. She then programs a yellow square with the name of another character from the story. On each square, she lists ways each character is different from the other. Then, on the green square, the student lists ways the two characters are similar. Finally, she glues the three squares to a sheet of construction paper as shown.

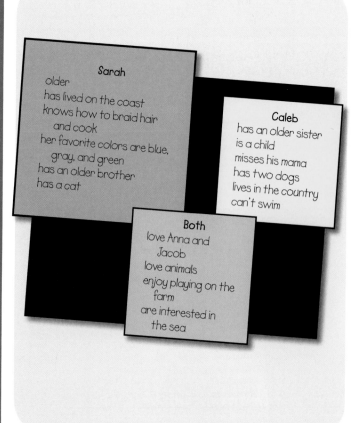

Sarah
older
has lived on the coast
knows how to braid hair
   and cook
her favorite colors are blue,
   gray, and green
has an older brother
has a cat

Caleb
has an older sister
is a child
misses his mama
has two dogs
lives in the country
can't swim

Both
love Anna and
   Jacob
love animals
enjoy playing on the
   farm
are interested in
   the sea

Healing the Gaps

Transition words

Materials:
student copies of page 99
list of imaginary medical headlines
large index cards (four per student)
scissors
crayons
tape

> Possible headlines include "Splinter Removed From Roaring Lion," "Elephant's Allergies Cause Grief," and "Tiger With Toothache Seeks Care."

A student chooses a headline and writes it at the top of an index card. Next, she writes a way she would help the animal. On each of three more index cards, she lists an additional way she would help the animal. She then arranges the cards in order, colors and cuts out the bandages from page 99, and programs each bandage with an appropriate transition word or phrase to use between each card. Finally, with the bandages and cards in order, she tapes them together as shown.

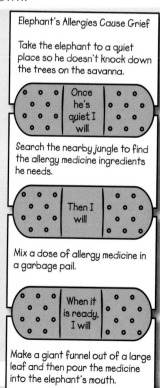

Zoom In

Narrative writing

Materials:
3 to 5 recently read fiction books
paper

A student selects a familiar book. He picks one event that takes place in the book. On his paper, the student then writes a brief but detailed story elaborating that single event.

Sam

Several years ago, Chester the cat was given to Mr. Monroe as a birthday gift. In the basket with Chester was the book *A Tale of Two Cities* by Charles Dickens. It was a lengthy car ride to Mr. Monroe's house, so Chester decided to skim the pages to see if the book was any good. After a few pages, Chester made a decision. Reading this book would be his new project for the week.

So every night after the family went to bed, Chester would curl up in a chair and read. He did almost nothing else. With only two pages left to read in the book, Chester was so tied up in his reading that he did not hear Mr. Monroe walk into the room. He was caught!

Chester thought for sure that this was the end of his stay in the Monroe house. But much to his surprise, Mr. Monroe was not at all surprised or upset to see his cat reading. In fact, he let Chester finish the final pages before sitting down to discuss the book with him. Mr. Monroe was so impressed by Chester's thoughts about the book, he began to ask for his feedback on other books and even his lectures for class.

Idiom Matrix

Idioms

Materials:
student copies of page 100
scissors
tape

A student cuts out the grid and cards and places each word card over the idiom it completes. Once all the idioms are covered, she carefully removes each card and writes the word on the grid in the space provided. Next, the student places each definition card over its matching idiom. Once all idioms are covered, she carefully tapes each definition card at the top to create a flap.

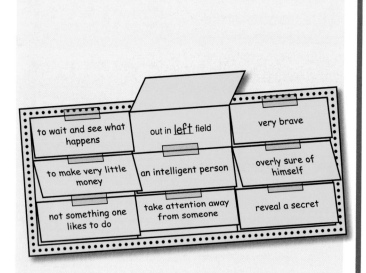

Fraction of a Notion

Making inferences

Materials:
magazine and newspaper articles mounted
    on construction paper and laminated
wipe-off marker
paper

A student selects an article, skims it, and circles its text features. Next, he writes the article's title at the top of his paper and lists several inferences about the article based on its text features. The student then reads the article and draws a star next to each correct inference he made. Finally, the student writes a fraction comparing the number of correct inferences to the total number of inferences he made. Then he wipes the marker off the article.

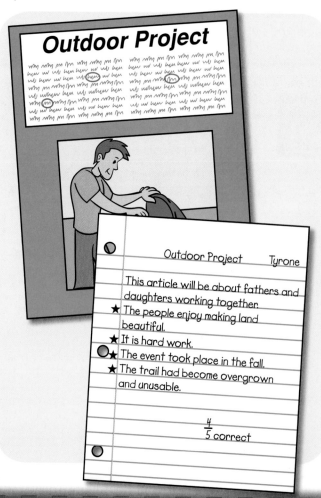

A Cut Above

Adverbs

Materials:
student copies of page 101
construction paper (one sheet per student)
highlighter
scissors
glue

A student cuts out the cards from a copy of page 101. Next, he sorts the words into sets by letter, arranges the words in each set to form a sentence, and glues the words to a sheet of construction paper. When he has ten sentences on his paper, he highlights the adverb(s) in each sentence.

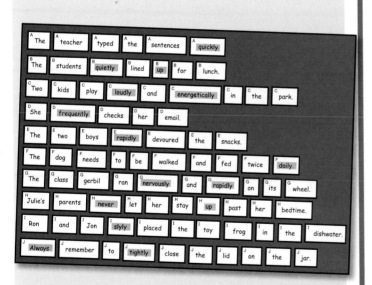

Stick to It!

Editing

Materials:
copy of the paragraph cards on page 102, cut apart
sticky notes cut into strips
paper

A student chooses a card and reads the paragraph. As she reads, she identifies any problems with the paragraph and marks them with a labeled sticky note. When she has finished editing the paragraph, she rewrites it on her paper according to the notes. She repeats the steps with each remaining card.

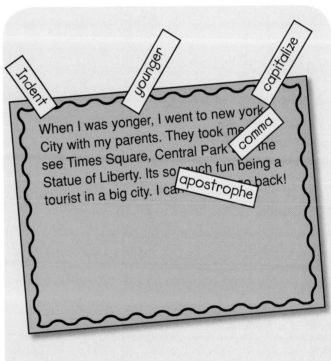

The Search Is On!

Dictionary skills

Materials:
student copies of page 103
dictionary
timer

A student uses the dictionary to complete the scavenger hunt on her paper as quickly as she can. As soon as she finishes, she records her time in the space provided.

Name **Lauren**   Dictionary skills

The Search Is On!

Use a dictionary to complete this scavenger hunt.

1. Find the name of an editor of the dictionary. **Frederick C. Mish**

2. Find a three-syllable word.
   decency

3. Find a word that has the prefix *mis-*.
   misquote

4. Find a word that has the suffix *-able*.
   forgettable

5. Find a word that has the root *mater*. **maternal**

6. Find a word that has a Latin origin. **language**

7. Find a word that has two or more entries. **light**

8. Find a word that has three or more definitions. **serious**

9. Find a word that has more than one pronunciation. **February**

10. Find a word that has at least one synonym listed in its entry. **circle**

11. Find a word that can be used as both a noun and a verb. **garden**

12. Find a word that has a Greek origin. **astrology**

Amount of time to complete: **6 min. 25 sec.**

Grab Bag

Facts and opinions

Materials:
magazines and newspapers
paper bag containing paper slips labeled
   "Fact" or "Opinion"
construction paper (one sheet per student)
scissors
glue

A student labels each side of his construction paper as shown and then draws a paper slip from the bag. If the slip says "Fact," he finds one fact in a magazine or newspaper, cuts it out, and glues it to the corresponding side of his paper. If the slip says "Opinion," he finds an opinion and does the same. He repeats this process ten times.

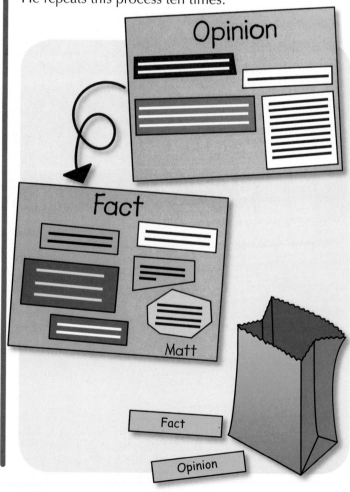

FANBOYS

Conjunctions

Materials:
newspapers or magazines
construction paper (one sheet per student)
highlighter
scissors
glue

A student writes the acronym "FANBOYS" down the left side of her paper. She then cuts from one of the periodicals a sentence that contains one of the seven conjunctions represented in the acronym. She glues the sentence next to the correct letter on her paper and then highlights the conjunction.

Karen

F ～～～～～～ **for** ～～～～～
A ～～～～～～ **and** ～～～～
N ～～～～～ **nor** ～～～～～
B ～～～～ **but** ～～～～～
O ～～～～～ **or** ～～～～～
Y ～～～～～ **yet** ～～～～
S ～～～～～ **so** ～～～～～

In the Routine

Explanatory writing

Materials:
paper

A student thinks of a typical classroom routine, such as turning in an assignment or lining up for lunch. On his paper, he writes an explanatory paragraph telling how to complete the routine in the most unique manner possible without breaking any classroom rules.

Seth

Lining Up for Lunch

We have been lining up for lunch the same way for years. I think it is time we try a new, more entertaining way of lining up. I like to call it the Texas Two-Step Lineup. To begin, a teacher uses her best Southern accent to start the process. As she calls each group to get in line, the students get in a single file and take two quick steps forward followed by two slow steps forward. The steps are repeated as many times as it takes the group to get in place. Each remaining group is called up in the same way. The class will want to say "So long" to our old routine!

Animal Antics

Similes

Materials:
copy of the simile list on page 98
paper

A student brainstorms on his paper a list of ten animals. He matches animal number 1 to simile number 1 and writes the complete simile on his paper. He continues in this manner with each remaining animal and simile. If a completed simile makes sense to him, he draws a star next to it. If it does not make sense, he chooses another animal to write in its place.

Similes

1. big like a(n) _____
2. worried as a(n) _____
3. busy as a(n) _____
4. quiet as a(n) _____
5. hungry like a(n) _____
6. ferocious like a(n) _____
7. lazy like a(n) _____
8. helpful as a(n) _____
9. crazy as a(n) _____
10. wise as a(n) _____

Tyler

	Animals		
★ 1.	tiger	1.	big like a tiger
2.	monkey	2.	worried as a ~~monkey~~ turkey
3.	kangaroo	3.	busy as a ~~kangaroo~~ bee
4.	anteater	4.	quiet as a ~~anteater~~ mouse
5.	bat	5.	hungry like a ~~bat~~ bear
6.	snake	6.	ferocious like a ~~snake~~ lion
★ 7.	dog	7.	lazy like a dog
8.	cat	8.	helpful as a ~~cat~~ dolphin
9.	elephant	9.	crazy as a ~~elephant~~ monkey
10.	llama	10.	wise as an ~~llama~~ owl

Getting to Know You

Character profiles

Materials:
student copies of page 104
colored pencils

A student completes a copy of the page as if she were the main character in a book she recently read. If some of the information is not presented in the book, the student uses her best judgment to make an inference about the character. The student then completes the page by drawing a portrait of the character in the space provided.

Name __Anna__

Getting to Know You

Name: __Lucy__
Age: __8 years old__
Birthday: __Feb. 12, 1938__
Hair color: __red hair__
Eye color: __green eyes__
Where are you from? __London, England__

Self-Portrait

Do you have any brothers or sisters? __Yes__ If yes, what are their names and ages?
__Peter, 13; Susan, 11; Edmund, 10__

What is your favorite color? __Red__
Who is your best friend? __Mr. Tumnus__
What bothers you the most? __when people accuse me of lying when I am not__
What is your favorite subject? __talking about Narnia__
What is your dream job? __being a queen in Narnia with my brothers and sister__

Rainbow Connections

Appositive phrases

Materials:
scrap paper
drawing paper
colored pencils

A student colors a rainbow on her drawing paper. Next, she writes a simple sentence on scrap paper. Then the student cuts the scrap paper so the subject and predicate are separate pieces. After she adds commas where shown, she trims each sentence part to make it look like a cloud and then glues the parts to opposite ends of her rainbow. Finally, on each rainbow band, she writes an appositive phrase that renames the sentence's subject.

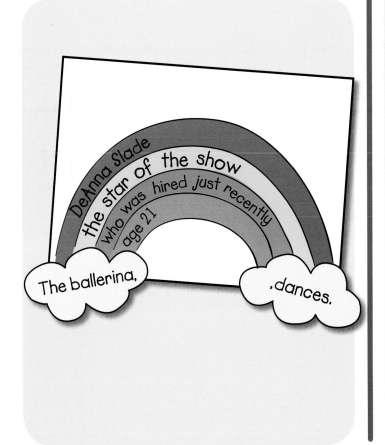

Official State Food

Persuasive writing

Materials:
drawing paper
notebook paper
colored pencils

A student thinks of a food he wants to be named as the official state food. Next, he writes a persuasive letter to his state representative explaining his reasons. The student then illustrates his version of the food as a symbol to submit with the letter.

> May 2, 2010
>
> Dear Representative Richards,
>
> I think our state should add a new symbol to its records. I believe we should have a state food, and I think it should be barbecue. I read in the newspaper that our state raises a large number of pigs that are used to make barbecue. The article went on to state the average number of pounds of barbecue eaten in a year by people in our state. Because of its popularity, don't you agree that it is time for this food to be recognized as a state symbol?
>
> Sincerely,
>
> Connor Payne

A Story of Opposites

Antonyms

For partners

Materials:
familiar picture books
sticky notes

Each partner selects a picture book and chooses words in his story that have opposites. For each word, he writes its opposite on a sticky note and places the note over the original word. When each partner has finished the story, the two students trade books. Each student then reads the new story and tries to identify the original word under each sticky note.

Whiteout

Making inferences

Materials:
child-friendly newspaper or magazine article
student copies of the article with the title, introductory sentence, and concluding sentence whited-out
highlighter
paper

A student places the original newspaper article facedown. She then reads her copy of the article and tries to infer the title, introductory sentence, and concluding sentence from what she reads. She writes her answers on a sheet of paper and highlights any text evidence that supports her answers. Then she looks at the original article to check her work.

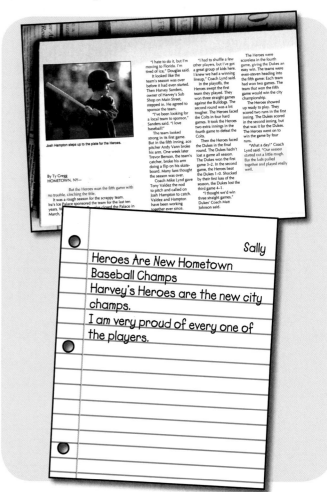

Boxed In

Syllables

Materials:
10–20 paper strips labeled with words comprising
    one to five syllables
dictionary
paper

Possible words include *shop, lap, yes, list, sun, action,
appeal, leopard, letter, broiler, important, imagine, imagery,
illustrate, immortal, calculate, imposition, identify,
remarkable,* and *origination.*

A student divides a sheet of paper to create five
rows and numbers the rows as shown. Next, she
places each paper strip in one of the rows according
to its number of syllables. After rereading each word
to check her work, the student sets the paper strips
aside. Then she uses a dictionary to find three
additional words for each category and writes her
answers in the matching row.

1 shop

2 appeal

3 calculate

4 identify

5 origination

Treasured!

Narrative writing

Materials:
student copies of page 105, copied on
    yellow construction paper
glue
paper

A student thinks of five things he wants and writes
each want on a separate coin pattern. Next, he cuts
out the coins and glues them along the bottom of a
sheet of paper. The student then writes an
imaginative narrative about finding his five wants in a
treasure chest.

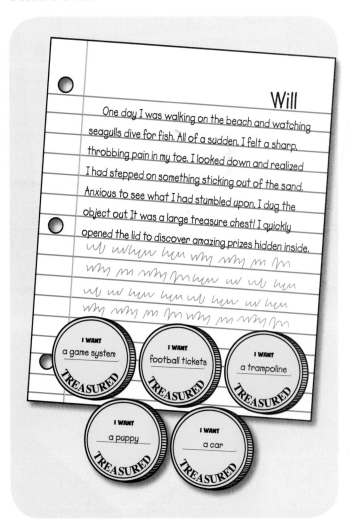

Will

One day I was walking on the beach and watching
seagulls dive for fish. All of a sudden, I felt a sharp,
throbbing pain in my toe. I looked down and realized
I had stepped on something sticking out of the sand.
Anxious to see what I had stumbled upon, I dug the
object out. It was a large treasure chest! I quickly
opened the lid to discover amazing prizes hidden inside.

I WANT
a game system
TREASURED

I WANT
football tickets
TREASURED

I WANT
a trampoline
TREASURED

I WANT
a puppy
TREASURED

I WANT
a car
TREASURED

A Million Times Better

Hyperbole

Materials:
familiar tall-tale books
paper

A student divides his paper into two columns and labels each column as shown. In the first column, he lists five events that take place in a tall tale of his choice. In the second column, he writes his own hyperbole, using an even larger exaggeration about the event. For added practice, the student turns his paper over, redraws the chart, and completes the activity again using everyday events instead of events from tall tales.

Event From Tall Tale	Hyperbole
Paul Bunyan gets ready in the morning.	Paul Bunyan uses a pine tree to comb his hair.

It's All in the Picture

Story retelling

Materials:
paper
colored pencils

A student divides a sheet of paper into six sections and labels each section as shown. After reading a story, the student uses colored pencils to draw pictures retelling a segment of the story under each label.

Pyramid Writing

Sentences

Materials:
paper

A student writes a one-word sentence toward the top of his paper. Centered underneath the first sentence, he writes a two-word sentence using the word from the first sentence and another word. He then writes a three-word sentence, adding to the two words used in the previous sentence. He continues in this manner until he reaches the bottom of his paper.

Eat!
Eat slowly!
Eat apples slowly!
Eat apples very slowly!
Eat sour apples very slowly!
Fruitworms eat sour apples very slowly!
Green fruitworms eat sour apples very slowly!

Paul

Petal Power

Descriptive writing

Materials:
colorful construction paper
large sheets of construction paper (one per student)
scissors
glue

A student thinks of a mystery object. Next, she cuts out a flower with five petals and uses her five senses to label each petal with a different descriptive phrase. On the back of one petal, she writes the name of the mystery object. The student then glues her flower to a sheet of construction paper, being careful not to glue down the petal with the answer on the back. She repeats this activity until her paper is filled with flowers.

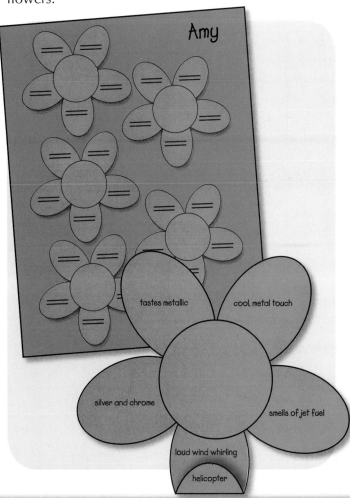

Amy

tastes metallic   cool, metal touch

silver and chrome   smells of jet fuel

loud wind whirling

helicopter

Sounds of Language

Onomatopoeia

Materials:
construction paper (one sheet per student)
markers

A student labels the front and back of a sheet of construction paper each with a different familiar location. The student then closes her eyes and recalls the different sounds she hears at each location. Then she writes on the corresponding side of her paper sound words heard at that location. If time allows, the student uses words from her lists in a story.

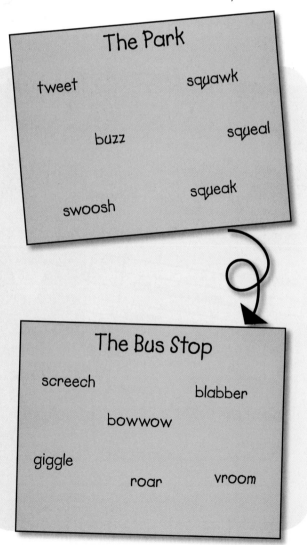

What a List!

Text features

Materials:
student copies of page 106
familiar books

A student selects a book. For each text feature found within his book, he places a checkmark next to it on the checklist. He then writes in the space provided an example of the feature or a page number where an example may be found. To conclude, he answers the questions about the importance of text features.

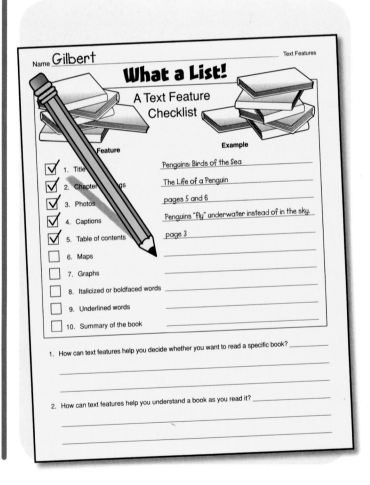

On the Fly

Conjunctions

Materials:
colorful copies of the butterfly pattern on page 107
    (seven copies per student)
list of conjunctions
books, newspapers, and magazines
scissors
glue

A student selects a text and scans the pages for sentences containing conjunctions. Once the student finds a conjunction, he records the sentence on a butterfly pattern, making sure to position the conjunction in the center of the body as shown. He continues in this manner until he finds all seven conjunctions from the list. Then he cuts out the butterfly patterns and staples them together to form a book as shown.

He
went
to the
office,

but

he did
not get
into
trouble.

Conjunctions
and
but
or
nor
for
so
yet

Doing Without

Explanatory writing

Materials:
paper

A student titles the top of her paper with a simple, everyday task, such as brushing her teeth or setting the table. She adds "Without a _____" to the end of her title, inserting the name of the most important element needed to complete the task. Then she writes an explanatory essay describing how to complete the task if the most important element suddenly was missing.

Sydney

Brushing Your Teeth Without a Toothbrush

To brush your teeth without a toothbrush, you must first forage a nearby park or wooded area for a small but sturdy twig. Make sure that your twig is not poisonous. Next, place a generous amount of toothpaste on one end of the twig. Gently begin to brush your teeth in a circular motion, taking care not to scratch your tongue or gums. Once you have brushed for at least two minutes, rinse both your mouth and the twig with fresh water. Save the twig for future brushings. Replace it when it begins to splinter.

Roots and Blossoms

Word origins

Materials:
copy of the root list on page 107, cut out
student copies of page 108
dictionary

A student programs the root of a flower with a root from the provided list. Next, she uses the dictionary to determine the origin of the root and the root's meaning. Then she writes her findings on the flower leaves. To complete her flower, she searches the dictionary and writes on the petals five words that are derived from the root. Then she repeats the activity with the remaining flower.

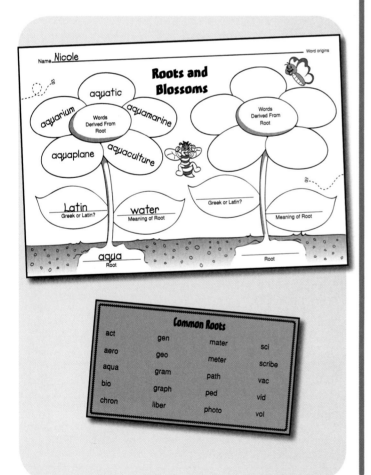

On the Hunt

Text evidence

Materials:
paper strips (five per student)
envelope or resealable plastic bag (one per student)

Each partner looks through a recent class reading assignment and writes on separate paper strips five questions that can be answered using text evidence. The student places his completed strips in an envelope and then he exchanges envelopes with his partner. Then each student reads his partner's questions and writes on the back of each strip the answer and page number or paragraph where the answer was found.

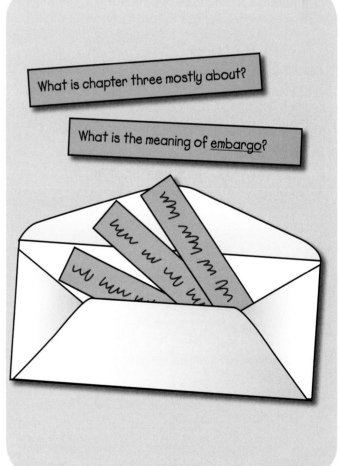

Grammatical Poets

Parts of speech

Materials:
copy of the poetry model shown
construction paper (one sheet per student)
scrap paper
colored pencils

A student follows the poetry model to create his own parts of speech poem on scrap paper. Then he neatly copies his poem onto the top half of a sheet of construction paper. To conclude, he draws an illustration of his poem on the bottom half of his paper.

Poetry Model

Noun
Adjective, adjective
Verb, verb, verb
Adverb
Modified adjective, noun

Matt

Beach
Sandy, balmy
Float, drift, bob
Lazily
Relaxing beach

Five Good Reasons

Persuasive writing

Materials:
colorful construction paper (one sheet per student)
scissors

A student traces her hand on construction paper and cuts out the resulting hand shape. Next, she thinks of something she might ask a friend to do, such as help her with homework or loan her a book. She writes the request on the palm of the hand cutout. Then the student imagines that her friend has said no to the request. To persuade her friend, the student writes five arguments in support of her request on the fingers of the cutout. She uses the resulting organizer to write a strong persuasive essay.

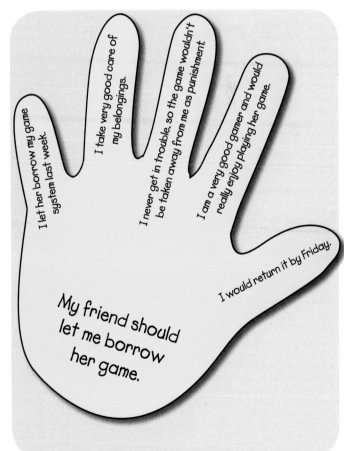

I let her borrow my game system last week.

I take very good care of my belongings.

I never get in trouble, so the game wouldn't be taken away from me as punishment.

I am a very good gamer and would really enjoy playing her game.

I would return it by Friday.

My friend should let me borrow her game.

Only Human

Personification

Materials:
common object (or a picture of one)
sticky notes (one per student)
paper

A student lists on a sticky note words that describe possible thoughts and feelings the object might have or actions it might do if it were human. Then, using her listed words, she writes a story about the object, having it act and behave like a human.

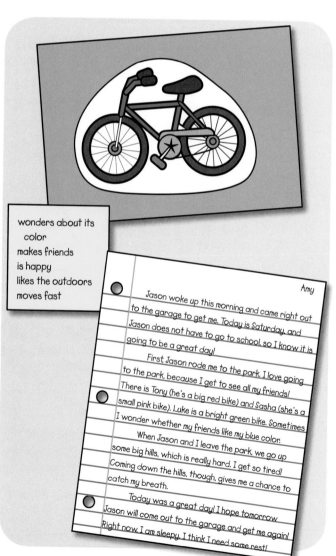

Focused on Details

Comparing and contrasting

Materials:
pair of similar pictures
construction paper (one sheet per child)

A child draws a Venn diagram on the construction paper and labels each section to represent one of the pictures. He brainstorms traits about the pictures and writes each trait in the appropriate diagram section.

Hunt and Highlight

Parts of speech

Materials:
newspaper articles
card labeled with directions, similar to the one shown
highlighter
paper

A student reads the directions on the card. Then she highlights in a newspaper article the specified number of examples of the featured part of speech. When she has found the appropriate number of words, she writes a sentence on her paper using each word.

Find ten verbs.

NEWS
Mavericks Win Big!

Tallulah

1. When I play games with my brother, I usually win.

Creative Cure

Explanatory writing

Materials:
craft sticks labeled with odd "ingredients", such as those shown, and placed in a plastic cup
paper

A child selects a challenge that he faces, such as having too much homework. Then he chooses three craft sticks. He writes an explanatory essay describing how the ingredients on the craft sticks will cure his problem.

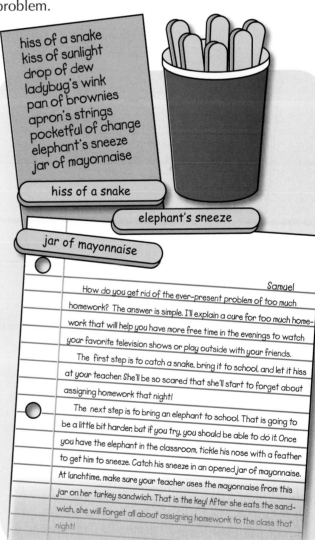

hiss of a snake
kiss of sunlight
drop of dew
ladybug's wink
pan of brownies
apron's strings
pocketful of change
elephant's sneeze
jar of mayonnaise

hiss of a snake

elephant's sneeze

jar of mayonnaise

Samuel

How do you get rid of the ever-present problem of too much homework? The answer is simple. I'll explain a cure for too much home-work that will help you have more free time in the evenings to watch your favorite television shows or play outside with your friends.

The first step is to catch a snake, bring it to school, and let it hiss at your teacher. She'll be so scared that she'll start to forget about assigning homework that night!

The next step is to bring an elephant to school. That is going to be a little bit harder, but if you try, you should be able to do it. Once you have the elephant in the classroom, tickle his nose with a feather to get him to sneeze. Catch his sneeze in an opened jar of mayonnaise. At lunchtime, make sure your teacher uses the mayonnaise from this jar on her turkey sandwich. That is the key! After she eats the sand-wich, she will forget all about assigning homework to the class that night!

If you follow these instructions precisely

What's That Word?

Spelling

Materials:
copy of the cards on page 109, cut apart
dictionary
paper

A child selects a card. He then uses the dictionary to find the correct spelling of the word and writes the word on his paper. The student continues in this manner until he has written the correct spellings of all 12 words.

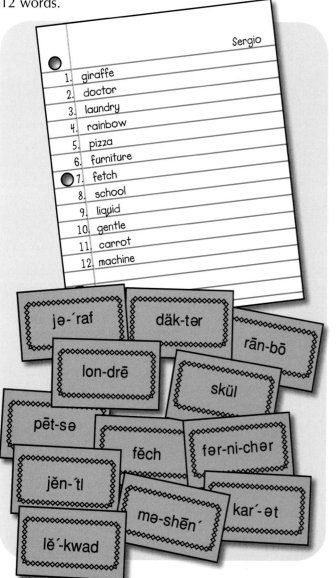

Read Me!

Genre

Materials:
construction paper speech bubbles, each labeled with a different genre (see the list on page 74)
paper

A student chooses two speech bubbles. She writes a conversation between the two genres in which each genre tries to convince the other that it is the better one to read. When she is satisfied with her dialogue, she asks a classmate to read the parts aloud with her.

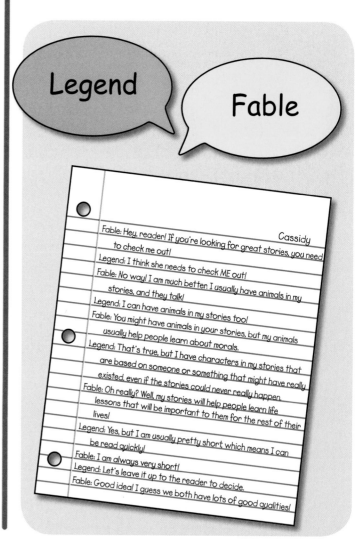

What's the Action?

Subject-verb agreement

Materials:
4 index cards labeled with singular subjects
4 index cards labeled with plural subjects
paper

A child divides his paper into four sections. He chooses two singular subject cards and two plural subject cards and labels each section of his paper with a different one of the chosen subjects. Then he brainstorms complete predicates that correspond to each subject and writes each one in the appropriate quadrant. As time allows, he repeats the steps by flipping his paper and selecting four different cards.

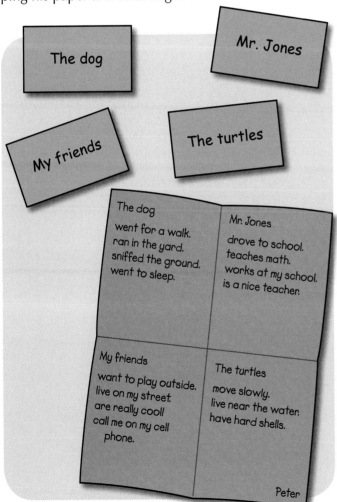

The dog

Mr. Jones

My friends

The turtles

The dog
went for a walk.
ran in the yard.
sniffed the ground.
went to sleep.

Mr. Jones
drove to school.
teaches math.
works at my school.
is a nice teacher.

My friends
want to play outside.
live on my street.
are really cool!
call me on my cell phone.

The turtles
move slowly.
live near the water.
have hard shells.

Peter

Catchy Commercials

Persuasive writing

Materials:
newspaper and magazine ads
highlighter
paper

A student selects an ad and highlights its critical information. Using the highlighted information and her own ideas, she writes a script for a radio commercial, persuading listeners to purchase the advertised product or use the advertised service.

Yummy Os!

A delicious and nutritious way to start the day!

Shonda

Good morning TZK listeners! Let me tell you about a sensational new breakfast cereal called Yummy Os. It is the best breakfast cereal to serve to your family. Not only is it delicious, but it is nutritious too! If you want to send your kids off to school with the best breakfast, serve them Yummy Os!

Set 35

What Does It Mean?

Multiple-meaning words

Materials:
copy of the multiple-meaning words from page 92
dictionary
paper
crayons or markers

A child chooses a word from the list and writes it on his paper. He uses the dictionary to determine the word's different meanings. Then he divides his paper so there is a section for each definition. In each section, he writes a sentence using a different word meaning and then illustrates each sentence.

Multiple-Meaning Words

ball	date	kind	point	sink
bank	drop	light	present	star
bark	face	like	press	stick
bat	fair	line	rare	story
bend	fan	mean	ring	tire
bill	file	mine	roll	trip
bowl	fly	miss	rose	vault
can	grave	order	run	watch
case	hide	pen	second	well
check	jam	play	ship	yard

Lloyd

jam

I put jam on my toast for breakfast.

My mom got stuck in a traffic jam this morning.

Be careful not to jam your finger in the door!

Packed With Facts

Research

Materials:
student copies of page 110
index cards labeled with research topics
several reference sources from which to gather facts
scissors

Possible reference sources include textbooks, nonfiction picture books, and encyclopedias.

A student chooses a card and copies the topic in the appropriate section of her box. She uses the provided reference materials to write a fact about the topic in each section. Then she uses the facts to write in the corresponding section a paragraph that describes her topic. Finally, she cuts out her box.

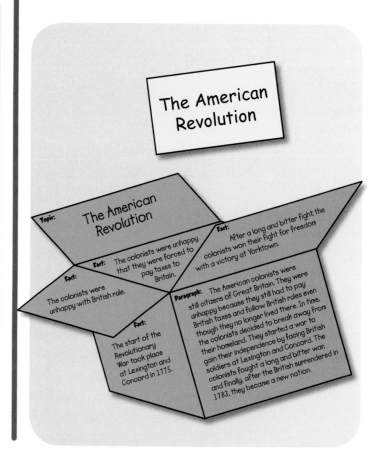

Orderly Sentences

Punctuation review

Materials:
bag of small paper squares, each labeled with a
   punctuation mark
paper strips labeled with unpunctuated sentences
paper

A student chooses a sentence strip and decides which punctuation marks are missing from the sentence. She removes from the bag the punctuation marks she needs and places them in the correct places. Then she copies the sentence onto her paper, adding the missing punctuation. She continues punctuating sentences in this manner as time allows.

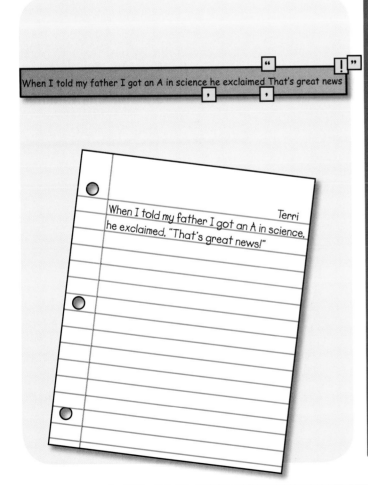

Sunny Weather

Argumentative writing

Materials:
large yellow circles (suns, one per student)
supply of yellow and orange triangles (sun's rays)
paper
glue

A child writes on his sun a statement telling how he feels about sunny weather. Then he writes sentences to support his statement, each on a separate ray. He glues the rays around the sun. Using the facts on his rays, he writes a paper arguing to support his opinion about sunny weather.

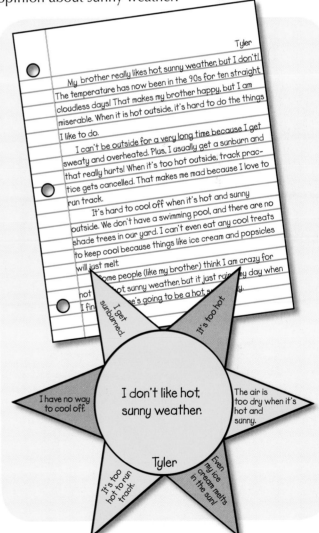

Vocabulary Creations

Prefixes and suffixes

Materials:
list of prefixes and suffixes on page 109
large index cards (one per student)
colored pencils or markers

A student chooses a prefix and a suffix from the list and adds them to a chosen word to create a unique word. He writes the word on his card and then adds a definition and an illustration.

Prefixes	Suffixes
ambi-: both	-ism: belief in, condition or act of being
anti-: against	
dis-: opposite of, not	-ite: one connected with
im-: not	
micro-: small	-logy: study of
neo-: new	-or, -er: one who takes part in
post-: after	
pre-: before	-sis: act of, process
pro-: in support of, forward	
re-: again	

antihomeworkism

The belief in being against homework
Thomas

Read It!

Genres

Materials:
list of genres (see below)
paper
markers

A child chooses a genre from the list and designs an advertisement explaining why people should read that particular genre. On the back of her paper, she lists examples of her genre that she would recommend to readers.

Genres

nonfiction
realistic fiction
historical fiction
biography
folktale
fable
fairy tale
fantasy
myth/legend
science fiction
mystery
poetry

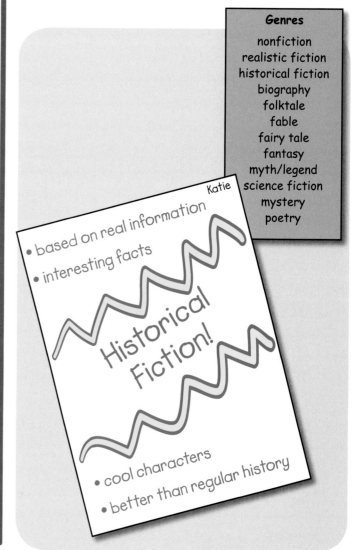

Katie

• based on real information
• interesting facts

Historical Fiction!

• cool characters
• better than regular history

Start the Same

Parts of speech

Materials:
index cards, each labeled with a different part of speech
index cards, each labeled with a different
    letter of the alphabet
paper

A student chooses a letter card and a part-of-speech card. Then he lists on his paper as many words of the chosen part of speech that begin with the featured letter as he can. When he cannot think of any more words, he chooses three words from his list and uses them to write a paragraph about a topic of his choosing.

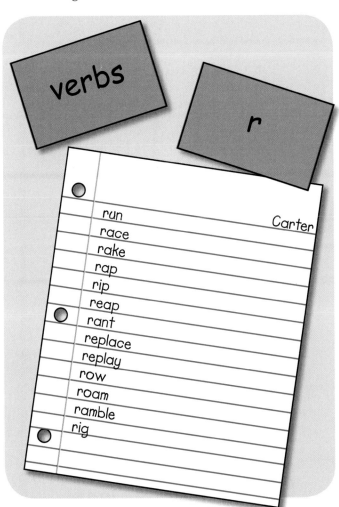

Ready to Work

Writing directions

Materials:
list of classroom jobs
index cards (one per student)

A child chooses a task from the list. She writes on her card a paragraph giving clear, precise instructions for how to complete the task. As time allows, she chooses a different task and writes another set of instructions.

Classroom Jobs

Board cleaner

Straighten book shelves

Push in chairs

Line leader

Teacher's helper

To clean the board, first take the markers off the ledge. Then spray the board with cleaner. Next, use paper towels to wipe the cleaner off. Make sure the board's surface is very dry. Finally, put away the cleaner and towels and return the markers to the ledge.

Marla

Direction Cards

Use with "Morphed Words" on page 4.

Begin with *MULE*.

1. Insert *BOBBLE* between the second and third letters.
2. Delete the first, fifth, ninth, and tenth letters.
3. Replace the last two letters with *RN*.
4. Switch the order of the third and fourth letters.
5. Add *ST* to the beginning.

TEC61151

Begin with *PROPER*.

1. Remove both *P*s from the word.
2. Add *ANN* between the second and third letters.
3. Remove the sixth and seventh letters.
4. Replace *A* with *U*.
5. Delete the first letter; then move the last letter to the front.

TEC61151

Begin with *DAISY*.

1. Insert *LOUD* after the first letter.
2. Move the fourth vowel to the beginning.
3. Replace the second letter with the eighth letter.
4. Replace *O* with the last vowel.
5. Delete the last letter; then change *U* to *N*.

TEC61151

Begin with *NOTEBOOK*.

1. Delete the first two letters.
2. Replace the second consonant with *A*.
3. Replace the last letter with *R*.
4. Insert *E* between the last vowel and consonant.
5. Replace the double vowels with *CH*.

TEC61151

Word Cards

Use with "Three to a Column" on page 6.

beast TEC61151	*break* TEC61151	*bunch* TEC61151	*clue* TEC61151	*crayon* TEC61151
crew TEC61151	*crime* TEC61151	*ditch* TEC61151	*glass* TEC61151	*grind* TEC61151
hatch TEC61151	*inch* TEC61151	*odd* TEC61151	*raft* TEC61151	*scold* TEC61151
shelf TEC61151	*shock* TEC61151	*sigh* TEC61151	*skill* TEC61151	*slope* TEC61151
speck TEC61151	*speed* TEC61151	*stain* TEC61151	*steam* TEC61151	*stock* TEC61151
stuck TEC61151	*suit* TEC61151	*throat* TEC61151	*trust* TEC61151	*west* TEC61151

Super Simple Independent Practice: Language Arts • ©The Mailbox® Books • TEC61151

rabid cat found in local park

wednesday nov 28

health officials said a rabid cat was found on the walking trail in lindley park tuesday and exposed an adult to the virus according to a press release from the feline county department of public health the cat tested positive for rabies

a health department spokesperson said that the adult who was exposed to the virus is currently receiving the rabies post-exposure vaccine series

health officials list this as the 21st case of rabies reported in the county this year and the third case involving a stray cat

for more information regarding rabies call the health department at 555-0177

Super Simple Independent Practice: Language Arts • ©The Mailbox® Books • TEC61151

Note to the teacher: Use with "Be the Editor!" on page 7.

77

Puzzle Cards

Use with "Make a Word!" on page 8.

un	QUESTION	able
	TEC61151	

un	FINISH	ed
	TEC61151	

re	PORT	er
	TEC61151	

un	FRIEND	ly
	TEC61151	

inter	NATION	al
	TEC61151	

de	LIGHT	ful
	TEC61151	

dis	APPOINT	ment
	TEC61151	

mis	LEAD	ing
	TEC61151	

dis	ORDER	ly
	TEC61151	

CARE	less	ness
	TEC61151	

POWER	ful	ly
	TEC61151	

DANGER	ous	ly
	TEC61151	

un	AFFORD	able
	TEC61151	

pre	MATURE	ly
	TEC61151	

mis	MANAGE	ment
	TEC61151	

Recording sheet

Word in the Spotlight

Name _____

Definition: _____

Word origin: _____

Synonyms: _____

Antonyms: _____

Sample sentence: _____

Super Simple Independent Practice: Language Arts • ©The Mailbox® Books • TEC61151

Note to the teacher: Use with "Word in the Spotlight" on page 10.

78

Silent *e* Words

argue	create	invite	please	store
believe	excite	late	pollute	survive
care	fame	life	refuse	televise
complete	guide	like	revise	use
confuse	hope	move	safe	value
continue	ice	narrate	shame	write

TEC61151

Suffixes

-able	-ion
-age	-ive
-al	-less
-ance	-ly
-ed	-ment
-er	-ous
-ful	-ty
-ing	-ure

Spider Pattern
Use with "'Spider-ific' Words" on page 18.

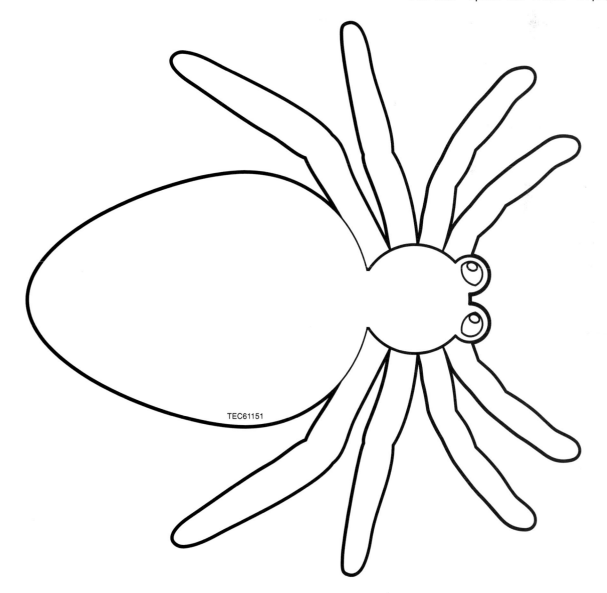

TEC61151

Commas in the Air

Circle each apostrophe in red or blue according to the code.

Code

Use of Apostrophe	Color
shows ownership	red
shows location of missing letter(s) in a contraction	blue

1. Each team's coach has to confirm the players' roster before the game begins.

2. It'll be nice to sleep in on Saturday morning instead of getting up for school.

3. Isn't Brian supposed to go to the dentist tomorrow?

4. Jessie's sister will be 16 on Wednesday.

5. Dad says we'll build a tree house once we're settled in our new home.

6. Did the neighbor's dog chew on Grandpa's work shoe?

7. Brad's bike isn't a ten-speed.

8. Can't we stop by the mall on the way home from Erin's house?

9. The girls' clothes got wet when Ian's glass of lemonade turned over.

10. Don't forget to study for the math test!

11. What's Sara's sister's name?

12. Kristin doesn't want to go to the movie unless it's over by 4:00 PM.

13. Mom says we're going to Disney World with Kevin's family!

14. That's a lot of pancakes to eat!

15. It's been two days since the storm hit our town, and the power's not back on yet.

16. There's a pile of clothes on my brother's bed that need to be folded.

17. If Uncle Glen's car won't start, how'll he get to work?

18. Haley's science book is on the table next to Mom's coffee cup.

19. Emma knows that she shouldn't eat anything made from peanuts.

20. The horses' saddles aren't supposed to be left in the barn.

Super Simple Independent Practice: Language Arts • ©The Mailbox® Books • TEC61151

Name _____

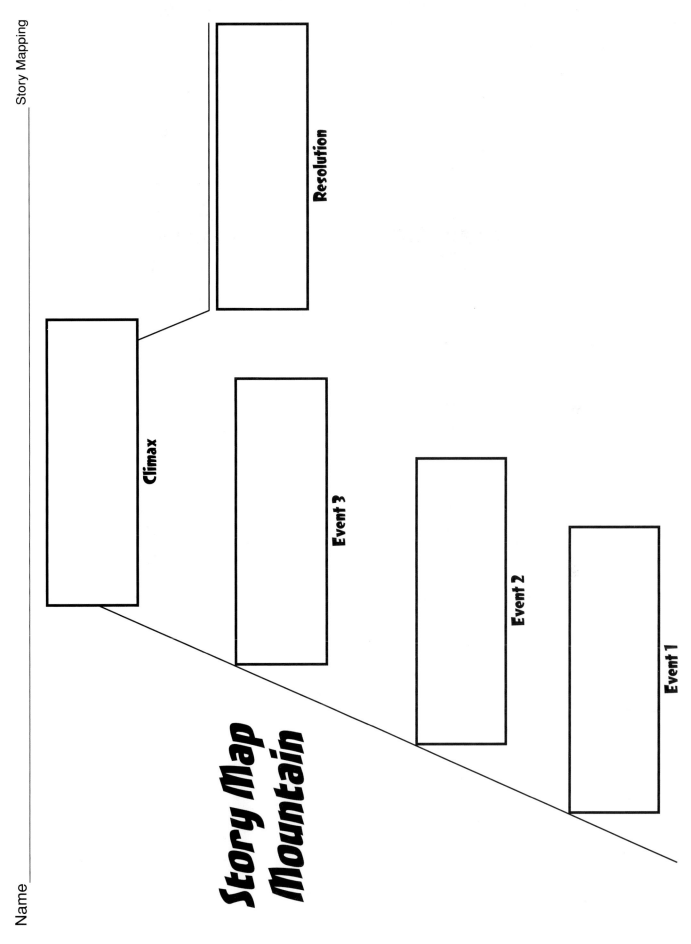

Resolution

Climax

Event 3

Event 2

Event 1

Story Map Mountain

Note to the teacher: Use with "Tell a Tale" on page 17.

Cell Phone Pattern
Use with "'Cell-ebrate'" on page 19.

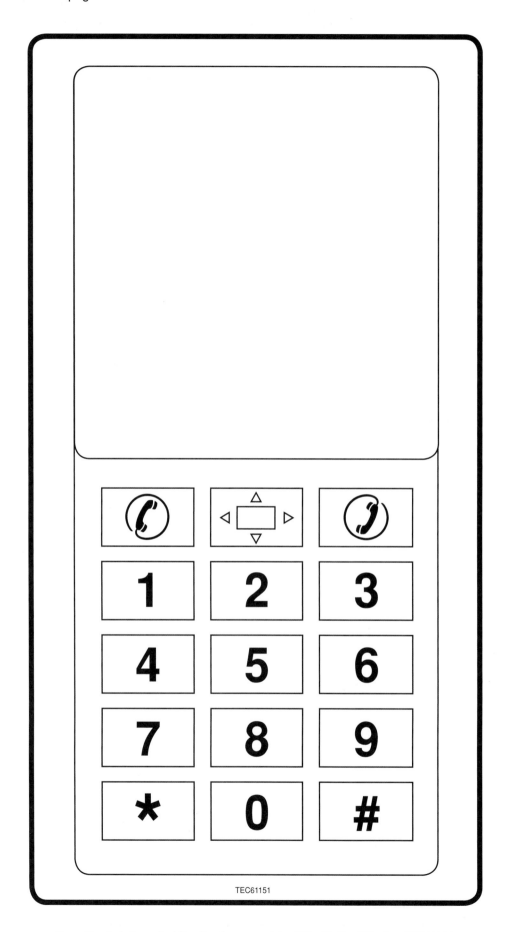

TEC61151

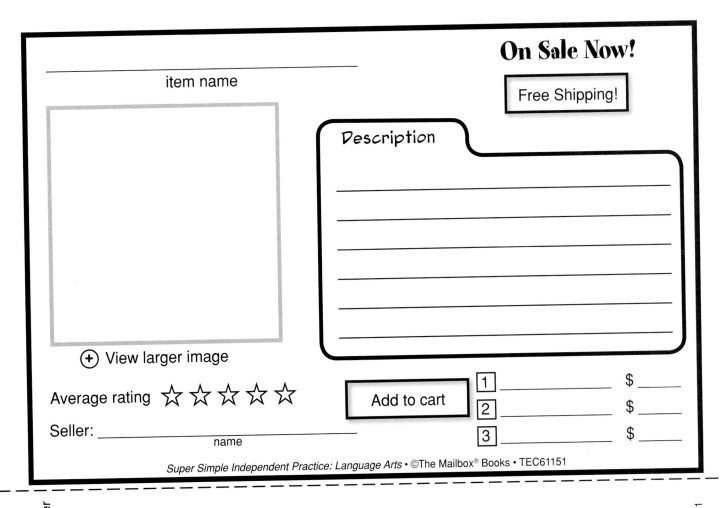

_____
item name

On Sale Now!

Free Shipping!

Description

_____
_____
_____
_____
_____
_____
_____

⊕ View larger image

Average rating ☆ ☆ ☆ ☆ ☆

Seller: _____
name

Add to cart

1 _____ $ _____
2 _____ $ _____
3 _____ $ _____

Super Simple Independent Practice: Language Arts • ©The Mailbox® Books • TEC61151

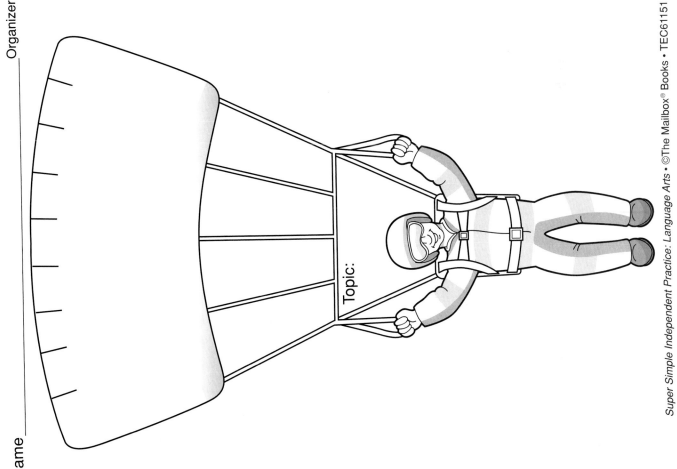

Organizer

Topic:

Name

Super Simple Independent Practice: Language Arts • ©The Mailbox® Books • TEC61151

Note to the teacher: Use the form with "Sale of the Century" on page 20. Use the organizer with "Open Up!" on page 21.

Story Cards

Use with "Short Story Sort" on page 20.

Spunky made room for herself. Before long, Spunky wasn't the tiniest or the weakest puppy in the litter.	It buzzed by her one time, two times, three times. She watched the bee, she snapped at the bee, and then she chased the bee.	Before she knew what had happened, she had chased the bee right off the back of the truck.	When it was time to eat, Spunky's brothers and sisters pushed her out of the way. So Spunky wiggled. Spunky squirmed.
She heard a reassuring groan. Spunky opened one eye and looked around. She sniffed. It wasn't a dream. It was her mom.	After a while, Spunky smelled a familiar smell. She felt familiar kisses.	She looked around. She sniffed. She whined. She dug a little hole and lay down in the cool dirt. Spunky whimpered; then she closed her eyes and fell asleep.	Spunky shook her head, looked around, and pawed her way out of the thorny bushes. She couldn't see the bee, the truck, or her family.
Spunky tumbled when she hit the ground, rolling over and over. When she finally quit rolling, she was dizzy and tangled up in tumbleweeds.	It was time to move to the ground where all the puppies could safely chase bumblebees and each other.	Spunky was born in the back of a pickup truck. Luckily, the truck had no tires, so it wasn't going anywhere. TEC61151	It was a good thing she was spunky too. One morning, Spunky caught sight of a bumblebee.
She was spunky though. That's how she got her name.	Spunky had four sisters and three brothers. Spunky was the runt: the tiniest, weakest puppy in the litter.	Spunky whined for a minute. She sniffed. She ran to the other side of the tumbleweeds.	Spunky was safe, and her mother realized it was time to move her puppies. It was time to move out of the back of the pickup truck.

Take Note!

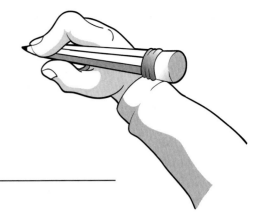

Record the title.
Write each paragraph's main idea next to a roman numeral.
Then write details that support each main idea.

_____
title

I. _____

   A. _____

   B. _____

   C. _____

II. _____

   A. _____

   B. _____

   C. _____

III. _____

   A. _____

   B. _____

   C. _____

Note to the teacher: Use with "Noteworthy Ideas" on page 22.

85

Comprehension Strips

Use with "What If...?" on page 24.

Choose an important event from Book 1. If that event took place in the setting of Book 2, how would the story change?

TEC61151

Choose an important event from Book 2. If that event took place in the setting of Book 1, how would the story change?

TEC61151

Name the problem in Book 2. How do you think the main character from Book 1 might have solved it?

TEC61151

Name the problem in Book 1. How do you think the main character from Book 2 might have solved it?

TEC61151

What if the main character from Book 1 became the main character in Book 2? How would the story change?

TEC61151

What if the main character from Book 2 became the main character in Book 1? How would the story change?

TEC61151

If the problem in Book 1 took place in the setting of Book 2, how do you think the story would change?

TEC61151

If the problem in Book 2 took place in the setting of Book 1, how do you think the story would change?

TEC61151

If the main character from Book 1 were a supporting character in Book 2, how would he or she act?

TEC61151

If the main character from Book 2 were a supporting character in Book 1, how would he or she act?

TEC61151

If Book 1 had the same mood as Book 2, how would the story change?

TEC61151

If Book 2 had the same mood as Book 1, how would the story change?

TEC61151

Late Again!

Cut apart the cards at the bottom of the page.
Glue each card in a box below to complete the paragraph.

When [ ] missed the bus this morning, [ ] knew [ ] parents would be mad at [ ]. John [ ] had already missed the bus two times this week! John's [ ] told him [ ] would not drive [ ] to school if [ ] missed the bus again. So [ ] started walking. [ ] walked to the home of [ ] aunt and uncle. [ ] was pretty sure his [ ] would drive [ ] to school if she had time. When [ ] knocked on the [ ], [ ] aunt and uncle met him with big smiles on [ ] faces. [ ] had already talked to John's [ ] and said she would drive [ ] to school. Aunt Tina made John promise to get up on time [ ] tomorrow. Then [ ] grabbed [ ] keys and drove John to school.

aunt	Aunt Tina	He	he	he	her	him	him	him	him	him	They	his	his
his	John	John	John	John	John	parents	parents	parents	she	she	they	his	their

Super Simple Independent Practice: Language Arts • ©The Mailbox® Books • TEC61151

Note to the teacher: Use with "He or Him?" on page 25.

87

Sock Patterns

Use with "Perfect Pair" on page 26.

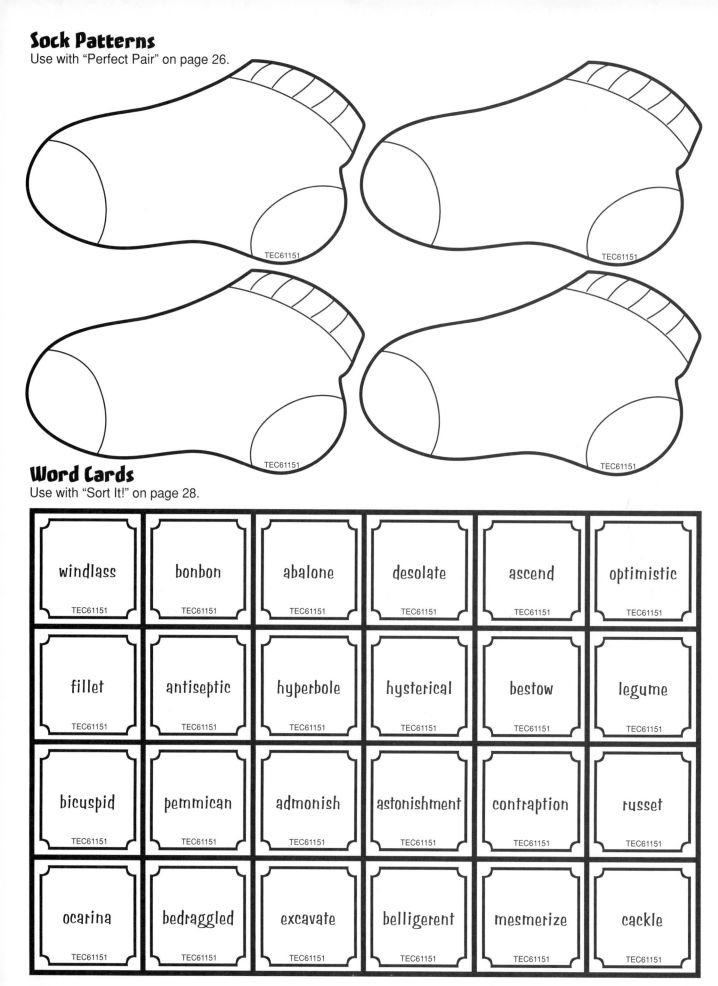

TEC61151

TEC61151

TEC61151

TEC61151

Word Cards

Use with "Sort It!" on page 28.

windlass	bonbon	abalone	desolate	ascend	optimistic
fillet	antiseptic	hyperbole	hysterical	bestow	legume
bicuspid	pemmican	admonish	astonishment	contraption	russet
ocarina	bedraggled	excavate	belligerent	mesmerize	cackle

Super Simple Independent Practice: Language Arts • ©The Mailbox® Books • TEC61151

Guide words

Follow the Guide

Before

Guide Word

Between

Guide Word

After

Super Simple Independent Practice: Language Arts • ©The Mailbox® Books • TEC61151

Note to the teacher: Use with "A River Run" on page 30.

Banana Patterns
Use with "Spelling Practice" on page 32.

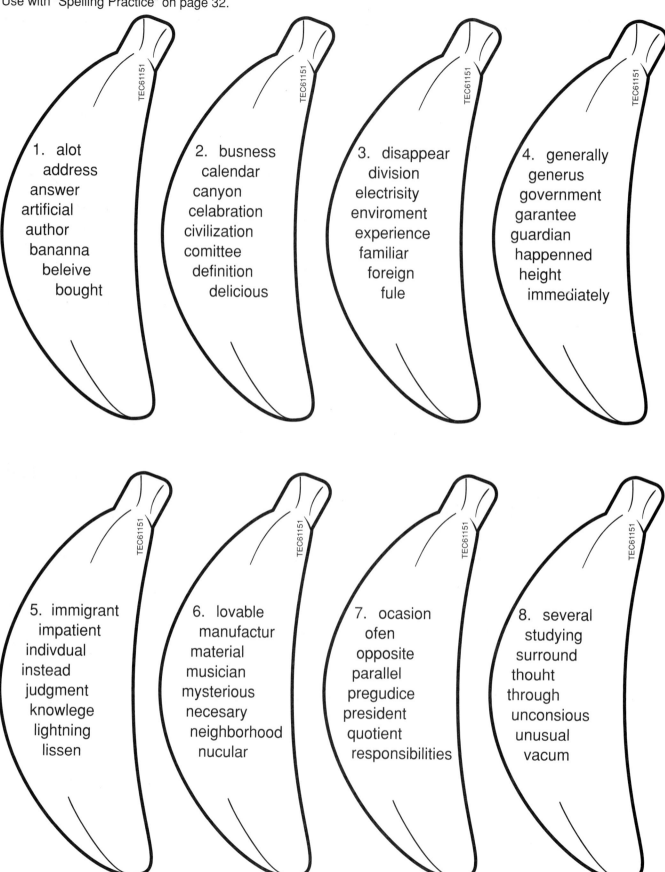

1. alot
   address
   answer
   artificial
   author
   bananna
   beleive
   bought

2. busness
   calendar
   canyon
   celabration
   civilization
   comittee
   definition
   delicious

3. disappear
   division
   electrisity
   enviroment
   experience
   familiar
   foreign
   fule

4. generally
   generus
   government
   garantee
   guardian
   happenned
   height
   immediately

5. immigrant
   impatient
   indivdual
   instead
   judgment
   knowlege
   lightning
   lissen

6. lovable
   manufactur
   material
   musician
   mysterious
   necesary
   neighborhood
   nucular

7. ocasion
   ofen
   opposite
   parallel
   pregudice
   president
   quotient
   responsibilities

8. several
   studying
   surround
   thouht
   through
   unconsious
   unusual
   vacum

I heard the new movie is fantastic. TEC61151

I can hardly wait to see the new movie. TEC61151

All my friends want to see the movie. TEC61151

I have to finish my homework and clean my room. TEC61151

We have practice at 5:00. TEC61151

I think I'll be riding with Jamie. TEC61151

I need to finish reading this book. TEC61151

I won't get my allowance in time. TEC61151

I think I just missed my bus. TEC61151

I've earned $25.00. TEC61151

I have seven more math problems to solve. TEC61151

The game starts at 7:00. TEC61151

Idiom Cards

Use with "Spiced Up!" on page 34.

apple of my eye TEC61151	boiling mad TEC61151	couch potato TEC61151	food for thought TEC61151
half-baked idea TEC61151	in a pickle TEC61151	other fish in the sea TEC61151	peas in a pod TEC61151
sinking your teeth into TEC61151	sly fox TEC61151	smells fishy TEC61151	stepping up to the plate TEC61151

Common Idioms

a bird's-eye view

a needle in a haystack

a piece of cake

bite the dust

blaze a trail

break the ice

catch your breath

everything but the kitchen sink

go overboard

hit the jackpot

hit the road

horse around

in a pickle

in the doghouse

in the long run

kick up your heels

lead the pack

make your mark

right up your alley

rolling in the aisles

take the bull by the horns

tough as nails

turn over a new leaf

walk on eggshells

with flying colors

Multiple-Meaning Words

ball	date	kind	point	sink
bank	drop	light	present	star
bark	face	like	press	stick
bat	fair	line	rare	story
bend	fan	mean	ring	tire
bill	file	mine	roll	trip
bowl	fly	miss	rose	vault
can	grave	order	run	watch
case	hide	pen	second	well
check	jam	play	ship	yard

Note to the teacher: Use the top list with "All About Me" on page 36 and "Similar Sayings" on page 44. Use the bottom list with "I Mean It!" on page 38 and "What Does It Mean?" on page 72.

Set A

Do	you	go	to	bed	early,	or	do	you	stay	up	late?

TEC61151

Set B

I	like	candy,	but	I	do	not	like	chocolate.

TEC61151

Set C

I	will	do	my	chores	first,	and	I	will	go	to	the	mall	after	that.

TEC61151

Set D

Carrie	is	still	buying	her	ticket,	so	we	have	time	to	buy	popcorn.

TEC61151

Name _____

Prefixes and suffixes

Oh, Brother!

Brothers can be such pests! Take my brother, for instance. His side of our room is unbelievably messy. He never picks up his things. His side of the floor is so unkempt that he cannot even see his feet once he sets them on the floor. His belongings have a way of creeping into my neat and tidy side of the room. Plus, any time something of his disappears, he tries to blame it on me. "I'm not the one who lives like a pig!" I always say.

Well, I have decided to teach my brother a lesson. Tonight, after he falls asleep, I am going to pile all his stuff into his closet. (The amount will likely reach the ceiling.) Then, when he wakes up in the morning and opens his closet door, an avalanche of clothing, sports equipment, and video games will fall on him. That ought to teach him not to leave his possessions lying around, don't you think?

Color Code
pink = prefix
blue = suffix

Super Simple Independent Practice: Language Arts • ©The Mailbox® Books • TEC61151

Note to the teacher: Use with "Highlight of the Day" on page 40.

93

Use with "Colorful Boxes" on page 42.

Board A

1. am	2. begin	3. eat	4. forgive
5. is	6. leave	7. read	8. shake
9. sing	10. slide	11. swim	12. teach
13. hear	14. shrink	15. write	16. catch

TEC61151

Board B

1. bite	2. blow	3. know	4. give
5. do	6. fly	7. hold	8. feed
9. feel	10. cut	11. build	12. ring
13. choose	14. forget	15. see	16. draw

TEC61151

Board C

1. break	2. dig	3. drive	4. fall
5. throw	6. freeze	7. go	8. lie
9. make	10. mean	11. rise	12. think
13. sink	14. wear	15. stick	16. win

TEC61151

Answer Key

Board A
1. was, been
2. began, begun
3. ate, eaten
4. forgave, forgiven
5. was, been
6. left, left
7. read, read
8. shook, shaken
9. sang, sung
10. slid, slid
11. swam, swum
12. taught, taught
13. heard, heard
14. shrank or shrunk, shrunk
15. wrote, written
16. caught, caught

Board B
1. bit, bitten
2. blew, blown
3. knew, known
4. gave, given
5. did, done
6. flew, flown
7. held, held
8. fed, fed
9. felt, felt
10. cut, cut
11. built, built
12. rang, rung
13. chose, chosen
14. forgot, forgotten
15. saw, seen
16. drew, drawn

Board C
1. broke, broken
2. dug, dug
3. drove, driven
4. fell, fallen
5. threw, thrown
6. froze, frozen
7. went, gone
8. lay, lain or lied, lied
9. made, made
10. meant, meant
11. rose, risen
12. thought, thought
13. sank or sunk, sunk
14. wore, worn
15. stuck, stuck
16. won, won

TEC61151

Going Around

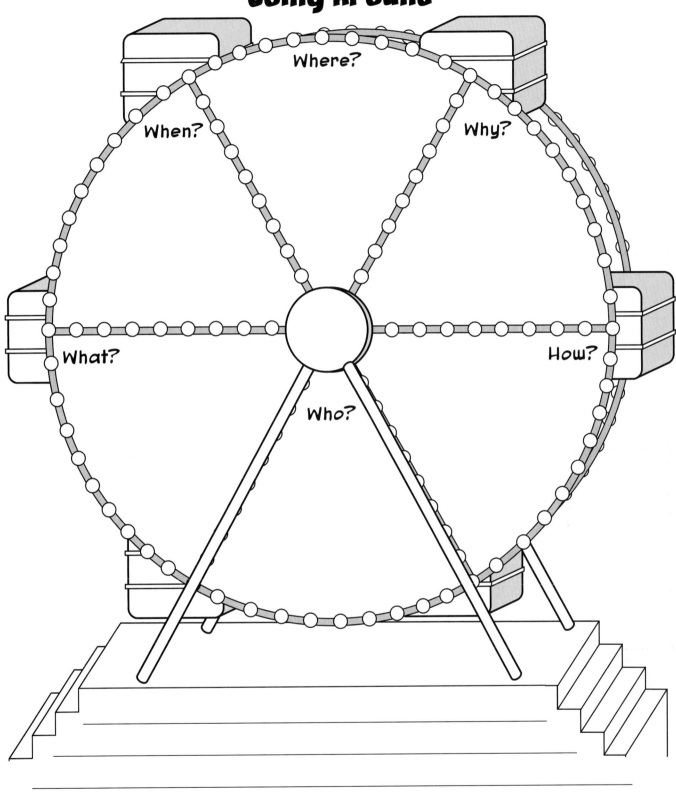

When? Where? Why? What? How? Who?

_____

_____

_____

_____

Super Simple Independent Practice: Language Arts • ©The Mailbox® Books • TEC61151

Note to the teacher: Use with "Now Reporting" on page 44 and "Here We Go!" on page 49.

Synonym and Antonym Strips

Use with "Same or Opposite?" on page 46.

synonym		word		antonym
		TEC61151		
synonym		word		antonym
		TEC61151		
synonym		word		antonym
		TEC61151		
synonym		word		antonym
		TEC61151		

Sequence Code and Sentence Strips

Use with "Roll and Write" on page 47.

Sequence Code

1 or 2 = beginning
3 or 4 = middle
5 or 6 = end

1. Nick's chocolate chip cookies tasted better than his mom's. TEC61151

2. Ten bald eagles landed on the beach. TEC61151

3. Stacy could hardly wait to see Aunt Bella. TEC61151

4. Megan wanted to be a test pilot. TEC61151

5. None of the technicians in town could fix Ben's laptop. TEC61151

6. A clap of thunder shattered the quiet of the campground. TEC61151

Graphic Recap

Use words and pictures to show the important ideas from your reading.

Title:

Homophones

add, ad	flower, flour	our, hour	shoe, shoo
air, heir	four, for	pair, pare, pear	so, sew, sow
already, all ready	heard, herd	peace, piece	some, sum
ant, aunt	hole, whole	plane, plain	son, sun
ate, eight	horse, hoarse	principal, principle	steal, steel
bare, bear	I, eye	read, reed	tail, tale
be, bee	made, maid	red, read	through, threw
blue, blew	meet, meat	right, write	to, two, too
brake, break	missed, mist	road, rowed, rode	toe, tow
by, bye, buy	need, knead	sale, sail	way, weigh
close, clothes	night, knight	see, sea	week, weak
dear, deer	no, know	sent, cent, scent	wood, would
die, dye	one, won		

Super Simple Independent Practice: Language Arts • ©The Mailbox® Books • TEC61151

Similes

1. big like a(n) _____
2. worried as a(n) _____
3. busy as a(n) _____
4. quiet as a(n) _____
5. hungry like a(n) _____
6. ferocious like a(n) _____
7. lazy like a(n) _____
8. helpful as a(n) _____
9. crazy as a(n) _____
10. wise as a(n) _____

Super Simple Independent Practice: Language Arts • ©The Mailbox® Books • TEC61151

Note to the teacher: Use the homophone list with "Just Joking Around" on page 52 and the simile list with "Animal Antics" on page 58.

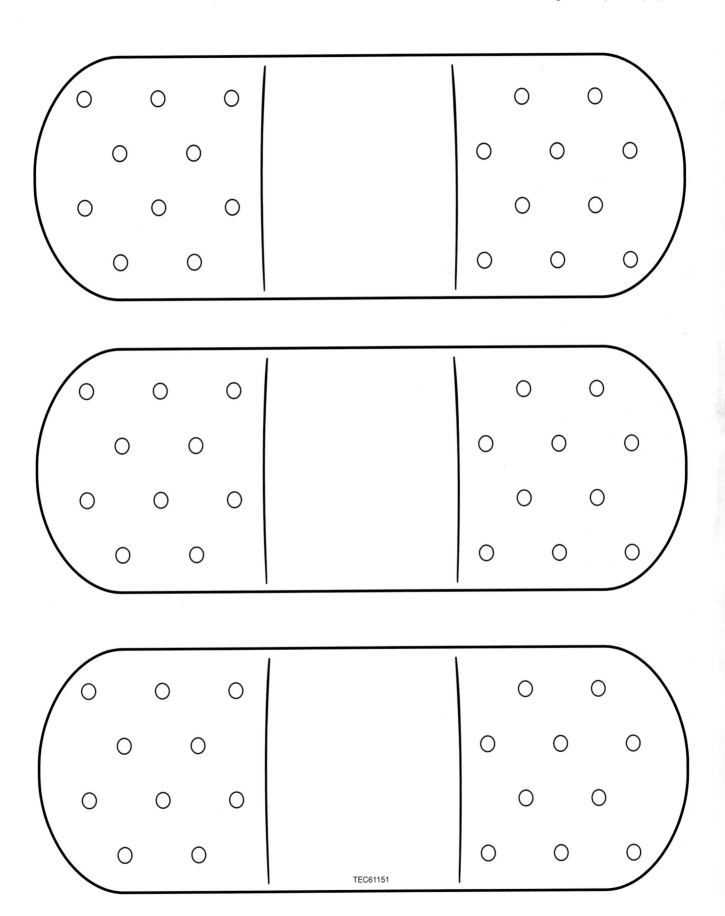

TEC61151

Idiom Grid and Cards

Use with "Idiom Matrix" on page 54.

play it by ____	out in ____ field	nerves of ____
working for ____	he/she is a smart ____	too big for his ____
not my cup of ____	steal someone's ____	don't spill the ____

TEC61151

peanuts TEC61151	ear TEC61151	britches TEC61151
beans TEC61151	steel TEC61151	thunder TEC61151
cookie TEC61151	left TEC61151	tea TEC61151

to make very little money	not something one likes to do	very brave
overly sure of himself	to wait and see what happens	an intelligent person
out of the ordinary	take attention away from someone	reveal a secret

A quickly.	J on	H her	I Jon	I in	C park.	D email.

TEC61151

C energetically	I slyly	E rapidly	C in	F The	C and

A The	B up	H let	F to	H Julie's	G on	B The	H stay	H her

H up	B lined	B students	J tightly	H parents	E two

D frequently	C the	C play	I the	I placed	E boys

I dishwater.	J close	E snacks.	J remember	I Ron

H never	E devoured	B lunch.	F walked	G nervously

C loudly	D her	A sentences	G its	G wheel.	G gerbil

J Always	H past	G The	F daily.	H bedtime.	B quietly

A teacher	A the	J jar.	G class	D checks	G ran	J lid

G rapidly	G and	F dog	D She	A typed	F and	F needs

I frog	E the	F twice	I and	E The	C kids	J the

I the	F fed	F be	B for	J to	J the	C Two	I toy

Paragraph Cards

Use with "Stick to It!" on page 55.

I think that student's should be given time at school to finish there homework. By the time we get home in the afternoon all we want to do is play relax, and unwind. The last thing we want to do is to work for three more hours. I know that home work is important, but I also feel that relaxation time is important to. Don't you?

TEC61151

Billy was so excited to be in the sixth grad this year. That ment he could use a locker for the first time. one day, a very strange odor started coming from his locker. he didnt know what to do. So he emptied out his entire locker. At the very bottom he found a stinky dirty old gym sock he had forgoten to take home.

TEC61151

When I was yonger, I went to new york City with my parents. They took me to see Times Square, Central Park and the Statue of Liberty. Its so much fun being a tourist in a big city. I can't wait to go back!

TEC61151

On saturday mourning, Kate and her Mom went to the mall. Kate needed new shoes for gym class her mom needed a new vacuum cleaner. When they got to the mall the too split up to save time. Kate immediately went to buy the most coolest sneakers she could find. Her mom went to find the most powerful vacuum she could buy. They met back at the food court just in time for lunch.

TEC61151

Super Simple Independent Practice: Language Arts • ©The Mailbox® Books • TEC61151

The Search Is On!

Use a dictionary to complete this scavenger hunt.

1. Find the name of an editor of the

    dictionary. _____

2. Find a three-syllable word.

    _____

3. Find a word that has the prefix *mis-*.

    _____

4. Find a word that has the suffix *-able*.

    _____

5. Find a word that has the root *mater.* _____

6. Find a word that has a Latin origin. _____

7. Find a word that has two or more entries. _____

8. Find a word that has three or more definitions. _____

9. Find a word that has more than one pronunciation. _____

10. Find a word that has at least one synonym listed in its entry. _____

11. Find a word that can be used as both a noun and a verb. _____

12. Find a word that has a Greek origin. _____

   **Amount of time to complete:**

Super Simple Independent Practice: Language Arts • ©The Mailbox® Books • TEC61151

Note to the teacher: Use with "The Search Is On!" on page 56.

103

Name _____

Getting to Know You

Name: _____

Age: _____

Birthday: _____

Hair color: _____

Eye color: _____

Where are you from? _____

_____

| |
| Self-Portrait |

Do you have any brothers or sisters? _____ If yes, what are their names and ages?

_____

_____

What is your favorite color? _____

Who is your best friend? _____

What bothers you the most? _____

_____

What is your favorite subject? _____

What is your dream job? _____

Super Simple Independent Practice: Language Arts • ©The Mailbox® Books • TEC61151

104 **Note to the teacher:** Use with "Getting to Know You" on page 58.

What a List!

A Text Feature Checklist

	Text Feature	Example
☐	1. Title	_____
☐	2. Chapter headings	_____
☐	3. Photos	_____
☐	4. Captions	_____
☐	5. Table of contents	_____
☐	6. Maps	_____
☐	7. Graphs	_____
☐	8. Italicized or boldfaced words	_____
☐	9. Underlined words	_____
☐	10. Summary of the book	_____

1. How can text features help you decide whether you want to read a specific book? _____

_____

_____

2. How can text features help you understand a book as you read it? _____

_____

_____

Super Simple Independent Practice: Language Arts • ©The Mailbox® Books • TEC61151

106 **Note to the teacher:** Use with "What a List!" on page 64.

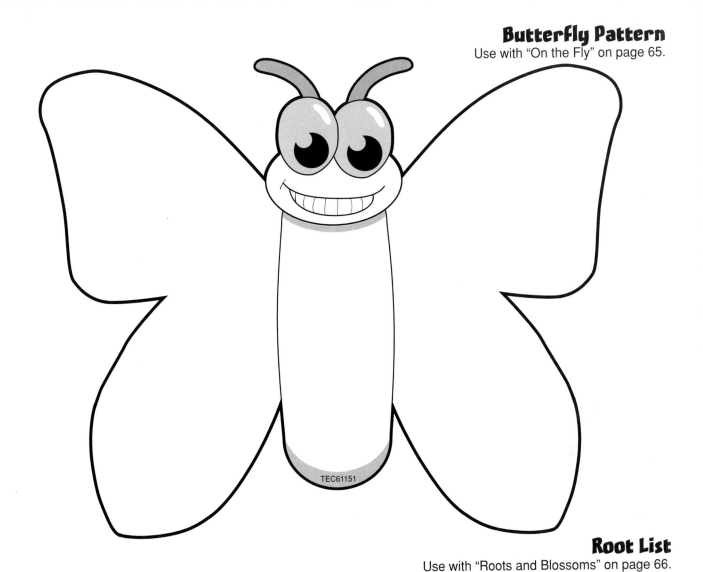

TEC61151

Root List
Use with "Roots and Blossoms" on page 66.

Common Roots

act	gen	mater	sci
aero	geo	meter	scribe
aqua	gram	path	vac
bio	graph	ped	vid
chron	liber	photo	vol

TEC61151

Name _____

108

Roots and Blossoms

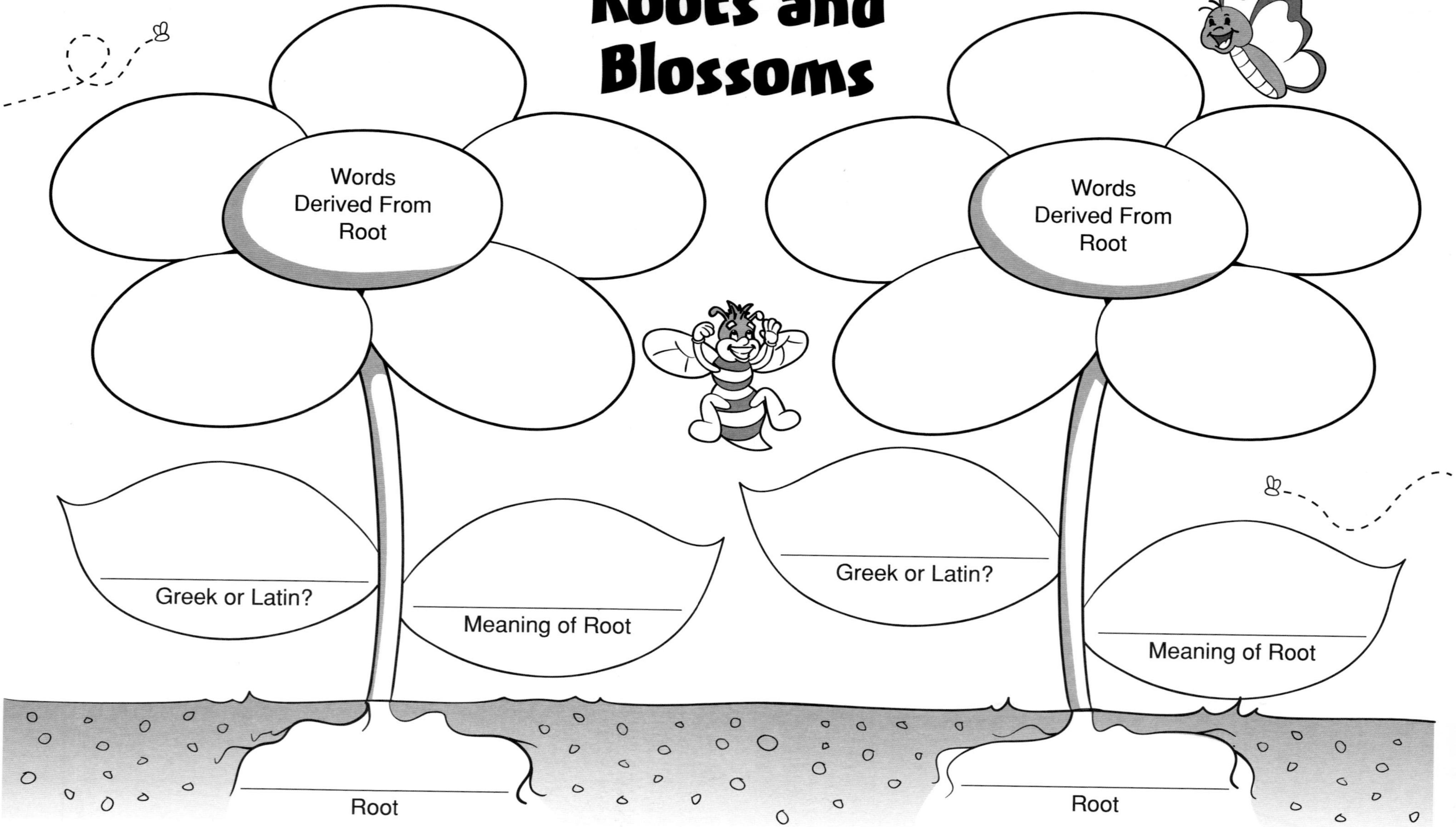

Words Derived From Root

Greek or Latin?

Meaning of Root

Root

Words Derived From Root

Greek or Latin?

Meaning of Root

Root

Note to the teacher: Use with "Roots and Blossoms" on page 66.

jə-ˈraf	ˈdäk-tər	ˈrān-bō
TEC61151	TEC61151	TEC61151
ˈlȯn-drē	ˈpēt-sə	ˈfər-ni-chər
TEC61151	TEC61151	TEC61151
fĕch	skül	ˈlĕ-kwəd
TEC61151	TEC61151	TEC61151
ˈjĕn-tl	ˈkar-ət	mə-ˈshēn
TEC61151	TEC61151	TEC61151

Prefixes	Suffixes
ambi– : both	-ism: belief in, condition or act of being
anti– : against	
dis– : opposite of, not	-ite: one connected with
im– : not	
micro– : small	-logy: study of
neo– : new	-or, -er: one who takes part in
post– : after	
pre– : before	-sis: act of, process
pro– : in support of, forward	
re– : again	

TEC61151

Note to the teacher: Use with "Vocabulary Creations" on page 74.

Box Pattern

Use with "Packed With Facts"
on page 72.

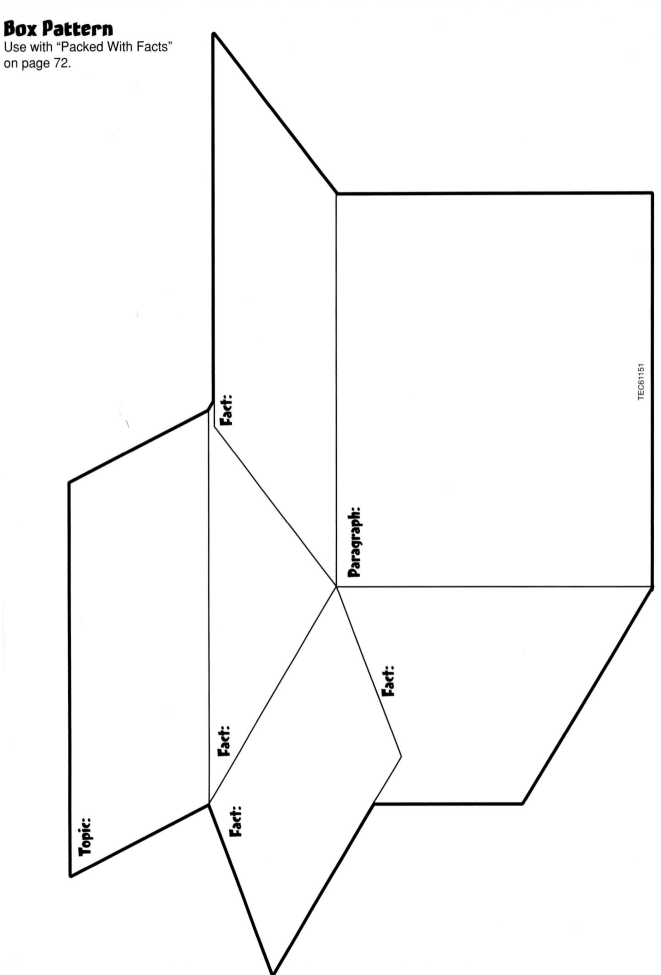

Skills Index